Biblical Approaches
to Pastoral Counseling

Books by Donald Capps
Published by The Westminster Press

Biblical Approaches to Pastoral Counseling

Pastoral Care: A Thematic Approach

*Pastoral Counseling and Preaching:
A Quest for an Integrated Ministry*

Biblical Approaches to Pastoral Counseling

by
Donald Capps

The Westminster Press
Philadelphia

BOOK DESIGN BY ALICE DERR

First edition

Published by The Westminster Press®
Philadelphia, Pennsylvania

PRINTED IN THE UNITED STATES OF AMERICA
9 8 7 6 5 4 3 2 1

Library of Congress Cataloging in Publication Data

Capps, Donald.
    Biblical approaches to pastoral counseling.

    Includes bibliographical references.
    1. Pastoral counseling. 2. Bible—Criticism,
interpretation, etc. I. Title.
BV4012.2.C26   253.5   81–11473
ISBN 0–664–24388–6   AACR2

To Mildred and Holden
　　Psalm 16:6

Contents

Introduction

Christians have always looked to the Bible for help in solving their problems. Yet the role of the Bible in pastoral counseling is a controversial issue. There has been much discussion, even heated argument, over such questions as: Should the Bible be quoted or read during counseling? If so, under what conditions? Does its use depend on who the counselee is, or what the counselee's problem is? Are there situations in which the use of the Bible is inappropriate? Does its use threaten to turn counseling into Bible study or preaching?

Others ask: Is the overt use of the Bible its only possible role in counseling? Might the Bible inform pastoral counseling without actually being used in counseling? If so, how might this occur? Is it a matter of allowing the Bible to guide the counselor's thoughts? Or does the Bible inform counseling in a more systematic or structured way? If so, how is this done?

These questions, and many others like them, have been raised in the seminary classroom, in the context of clinical pastoral education, in pastoral counseling centers, and in the local church setting. A number of books and articles have been written on the topic. Workshops, symposiums, and panel discussions have been devoted to it. Yet a great deal of uncertainty and ambiguity about the issue remains. There seems to be broad agreement among ministers that the Bible has a role to play in pastoral counseling, but there is little consensus about what this role should be. Some books on pastoral counseling develop a model of "biblical" or "scriptural" counseling. Other books see the Bible primarily as a valuable "religious resource" along with prayer and other devotional literature. Still other books fail to provide a role for the Bible at all.

This literature undoubtedly reflects the range of actual practice. Some ministers see the Bible providing the overall framework for counseling. For them, the problems of the counselee need to be treated from a "biblical perspective" because the Bible is adequate to deal with any and all problems that parishioners bring to their pastors. Other ministers are reluctant to call their counseling "biblical counseling," but they are able to cite various instances when their counseling was informed by biblical understandings. Still other ministers resist the idea that the Bible might have a role in pastoral counseling. Some of them are concerned about the abuses that may result from an irresponsible use of the Bible, others believe that its use inhibits the effectiveness of counseling, and still others simply believe that the Bible is not very relevant to the problems they deal with in their counseling.

It is unlikely that a consensus on the role of the Bible in pastoral counseling can be reached, given the wide range of views and attitudes about it. But we can achieve much greater clarity than we have to date about this important issue, and this book is meant to make a contribution toward such clarification.

My approach to this issue is twofold. First, I believe it is important to review the work that has been done on the subject. There is already an extensive literature on this topic that represents a broad spectrum of viewpoints. In Chapter

1, I discuss this literature, identifying the major perspectives. But clarity on the issue will not come solely from reviewing this material. The existing literature reflects so many different viewpoints, some conflicting, that it confuses as well as enlightens. So, a second strategy of this book is to bring insights from modern biblical scholarship to bear on the issue.

In surveying the literature on the use of the Bible in pastoral counseling, I have been struck by the fact that contemporary biblical studies have not informed these discussions to any appreciable degree. Some authors voice their support of modern methods of biblical research, while others castigate these methods, but the writings of biblical scholars are rarely cited by either camp. It is not difficult to understand why this is the case. Biblical studies have become the work of specialists, and their writings are often too technical or too narrowly focused to seem of value to pastoral counseling. A related problem is that biblical studies are a large enterprise, and it is not always easy to identify, out of this vast literature, the studies that promise to be most useful to pastoral counseling. The sheer scope and complexity of biblical scholarship tends to intimidate those who represent the practical theological disciplines. As a result, books and articles on the Bible's role in pastoral counseling are generally uninformed by relevant biblical scholarship.

Once one decides to apply modern biblical studies to pastoral counseling, a difficult question is, How can one make such application? One might study the counseling practices of such biblical figures as Samuel, the prophets, Jesus, or Paul. Or one might explore the biblical treatment of theological problems that are frequently mentioned in modern counseling, such as evil and suffering. In my view, however, a particularly valuable approach is to use the recognition that the Bible is composed of a variety of literary forms, and to explore the different ways these forms are significant in pastoral

counseling. Often circulated orally before being written and
incorporated into biblical texts, the forms include sagas, folk
tales, legends, prophetic and apocalyptic sayings, legal codes,
proverbs, hymns, laments, parables, letters, and many, many
others. Acknowledgment of this diversity can help one to
avoid the mistake of looking legalistically to the Bible as a
simple rule book.

Not all of these forms are directly relevant to pastoral
counseling, but some definitely are. In this book, I will focus
on three of these forms—psalms, proverbs, and parables.

In Chapters 2 to 4, I will be discussing in detail how these
three biblical forms may help to clarify and achieve the objectives of pastoral counseling. But I would like to comment
briefly here on the general approach of this book in order to
give the reader a foretaste of what is to come.

THE APPROACH OF THIS BOOK

The question is not whether the Bible has a role in pastoral
counseling, but what is the nature of this role? The approach
developed in this book is based on the premise that, in order
to clarify the role of the Bible in pastoral counseling, we need
to turn to modern biblical scholarship, especially to what is
commonly called "form criticism."

Form criticism is one of three related disciplines in modern
biblical criticism: literary criticism, form criticism, and
redaction criticism. Literary criticism identifies smaller literary units that comprise a biblical book and seeks to explain
them in terms of separate sources, not always doing so with
success. Form criticism shifts from sources to an identification of units in terms of form or literary genre, such as saga,
folk tale, legend, or prophetic saying. This method tries to
discern the original religious and social needs which the units
served, often in a presumed preliterary stage. It is noteworthy
that the three forms emphasized in this study—psalms, pro-

verbs, and parables—were suited to oral communication. Most recently, redaction criticism has tried to discern how small traditional units were assembled into larger complexes, particularly how collections expressed theological themes.

This book approaches biblical material as form criticism does, concentrating on psalms, proverbs, and parables. Like form critics, we will ask questions about their origins, with the conviction that the human needs and problems which the material expresses have great relevance today. Clearly, the psalms, like most poetry, served to express a variety of emotions, perhaps within a liturgical context. The proverbs, like most sayings, were intended for teaching, particularly the communication of moral truths. Parables, as narrative, were suited for teaching that concerned action, change, and transformation. The similarities in the purposes of these forms and the uses of the Bible in pastoral counseling should not surprise us, for the basic socioreligious needs of individuals have remained relatively constant through the centuries, as has the role of religious institutions in addressing these needs. As anthropologist Clifford Geertz has pointed out, the three major types of existential situations that religion addresses are those which force us to the limits of our endurance (the problem of suffering), those which press the limits of our moral insight (the problem of evil), and those which reveal the limits of our comprehension (the problem of metaphysical anxiety).[1] The three biblical forms that we are concerned with in this book relate to these three limit situations, with the psalm addressing the limits of our endurance (and need for comfort), the proverb addressing the limits of our moral insight (and need for instruction), and the parable concerned with the limits of human comprehension (and need for reinterpretation and diagnostic assessment). The structure of these formal units may also have significance for pastoral counseling. We will see shortly, for instance, that the parts of a psalm of lament correspond to the successive phases of grief counseling.

Counseling methods differ with each of the different forms, all having as their basic objective a change in the person being counseled. With psalms, nondirective methods are best used, with the change initiated through the expression of feelings. The counselor's role is to help clarify the feelings. The proverb encourages a more directive method, with the focus of change being the individual's moral behavior. The counselor provides moral direction and guidance. The parable invites a more indirective method, with the change it fosters being primarily perceptual in nature. The counselor acts as reinterpreter.

This book will show how each of these literary forms from the Bible is related to counseling individuals who are facing a specific situation. Clearly the psalms express a wide range of feelings, but we will explore here principally the ways in which some psalms of lament may help those who are grieving. Similarly, proverbs address a vast array of human problems, but here we emphasize their relevance to the counseling of persons who are about to be married, who are in need of moral instruction. Likewise, parables deal with a range of issues, but the perceptual restructuring they encourage can be especially valuable to persons seeking help for troubled marriages. These three particular types of situations are very frequently encountered by pastors, who may wish for specifically biblical resources in their counseling ministry.

My undertaking has its risks. Each of these literary forms exists in great variety and has been the subject of considerable scholarly attention. I have attempted to familiarize myself with much of the significant biblical scholarship on these three forms, but there are undoubtedly many important books and articles that I have missed. Also, I have needed to be highly selective in my choice of materials for actual discussion in this book. I have preferred to give a thorough treatment of a few authors rather than a cursory handling of many. This may mean that, in some instances, I invite the erroneous impression that particular views or ideas are unique to the biblical scholar I actually discuss, when they are in fact shared by many colleagues. Here, I ask the indulgence of the biblical scholar, since my concerns are not to trace the history of biblical scholarship on the psalms, proverbs, and parables, but to create a bridge between modern biblical scholarship and the practice of pastoral care and counseling. If I have made blunders in my interpretation of an author's views, or have failed to use the most relevant biblical scholarship available, I hope that readers will sympathize with the difficulties a nonspecialist confronts when dealing with three major areas of biblical scholarship. I have chosen to confront these difficulties, in spite of the risks, because any successful case for the Bible's role in pastoral counseling must include in its purview a significant range of biblical materials.

If the biblical scope of this book is large, the pastoral counseling focus is not narrowly construed either. The book is concerned with prescheduled counseling sessions in the pastor's study, but it is certainly not limited to these. I sometimes use the term "pastoral conversation" in this book to make the point that by "pastoral counseling" I mean to include hospital and shut-in visitation, pastoral conversations that occur over lunch, meetings with bereaved families before and after funerals, visits with married couples in their homes, sustained conversation with a troubled parishioner during the coffee hour after church or at a social gathering, a phone conversation with a distraught parishioner, or a "good talk" with a worried church member after a church committee meeting.

I want to express my appreciation to Dean James F. Caton and my faculty colleagues at The Graduate Seminary of Phillips University for making it possible for me to work on this book during the 1980–81 academic year at Princeton Theological Seminary. I also want to thank the Association of Theological Schools and the Lutheran Brotherhood of Minneapolis, Minnesota, for their financial support. A special word of thanks to my wife, Karen, and son, John, for their moral support.

D.C.

Chapter 1

The Bible's Role
in Pastoral Counseling

Much has been written about the Bible's role in pastoral counseling. There are many articles on the subject. There are books devoted exclusively to it, and most books about pastoral counseling include some discussion of it. This topic has had remarkable staying power over the last fifty years. It has gone into eclipse from time to time, but these periods of eclipse have been quite brief. At the present time, it is a prominent issue in pastoral counseling.

In this chapter, I survey this literature, discussing representative writings in roughly chronological order. It would be impossible to discuss all the significant articles and books, but these examples reflect the major theoretical and practical issues involved in clarifying the Bible's role in pastoral counseling. The counselor will find in this survey many practical suggestions for using the Bible. At the same time, the survey will show in what ways the approaches advocated in this book are significantly new. I will discuss the different phases in the development of this topic since the late 1930s. These include "emerging consensus," "European interlude," "conservative developments," and "moderate resurgence." I consider this study to be a contribution to the moderate resurgence.

EMERGING CONSENSUS

In 1936, Richard C. Cabot and Russell L. Dicks published their book, *The Art of Ministering to the Sick.* [2] One chapter in it, authored by Dicks, is devoted to the use of Scripture in the pastor's work with hospital patients. Dicks believes that prayer is the most important spiritual resource in work with the sick,[3] but he contends that the Bible is a valuable resource in support of attainment in prayer. When a sufferer does not want to pray, but wants to think or brood on important life-and-death matters, the Bible gives direction and purpose to such reflections, and thereby serves as a "spiritual training ground." Dicks points out, for example, that the Bible helps the sick patient to gain new perspectives, especially to begin seeing life steadily again. Patients who request a minister as they await surgery have recognized that "they needed the help of religion to gain a perspective from which they could view the experience they were facing. They need to see life steadily. They needed to have called to their minds the stability of God. 'I am thy rock and thy fortress.' "

The Bible also aids the sick in acquiring holiness. Biblical accounts of the difficult experiences of Jesus, Paul, Jeremiah, Amos, Hosea, and Job exemplify the achievement of holiness through perseverance in suffering. In Dicks's view, these biblical examples of holiness are especially valuable in ministering to the handicapped or physical disabled. But he does not explore this emphasis on holiness, or the idea that the Bible provides a means of gaining new perspectives, in any detail. Most of his discussion of the use of the Bible in pastoral care consists of recommended biblical passages for specific types of needs. Typical suggestions are Psalm 23 (for confidence), Psalm 121 (for strength), John 15:1–7 (for peace and quietness), and Matt. 6:25–27 (for release from worry).

While Dicks was concerned solely with ministering to hospital patients, he nonetheless set a precedent for viewing the Bible as an important "spiritual resource" in pastoral counseling. Pastoral counseling books published in the late 1940s and in the 1950s typically devote a chapter to spiritual or religious resources in pastoral counseling, with the Bible and prayer invariably included. Seward Hiltner's *Pastoral Counseling,* published in 1949, is an excellent example.[4]

Hiltner's chapter on religious resources in pastoral counseling includes discussion of prayer, the Bible, religious literature, Christian doctrine, and sacraments and rites. His major point in the section on the Bible is that its use should be consistent with good counseling principles. In evaluating a counseling session that involved exploration of the counselee's problems in the light of Psalm 38, Hiltner acknowledges that the pastor did some expounding of Scripture: "But, and this is what counts, he does not moralize, generalize, coerce, or direct. Instead he understands, accepts, clarifies, and helps to consolidate." In Hiltner's view, this pastor's use of the Bible was consistent with recommended counseling methods.

But Hiltner also cites a case in which the pastor violated this rule. This pastor noted that the counselee's conflict is "kind of like Paul—a war in your members." Hiltner says that such biblical references by the pastor "can be dangerous. Unless the reference is crystal clear, it would divert [the counselee] from his own situation to finding out all about why Paul felt that way; and before long [he] would have heard a good sermon but would have gotten no help on his own situation." Hiltner does not dispute the fact that the biblical reference chosen was relevant to the problem. Still, "this kind of approach should not be mentioned without a suggestion of its dangers, particularly the danger of distraction. The more interested the pastor is in the Biblical story or passage, the more likely is the parishioner to conclude that the pastor has taken the first opportunity to get away from considering his situation and onto familiar ground."

Hiltner's cautious view of the use of the Bible in pastoral counseling is also reflected in his comments on the practice, advocated by John Sutherland Bonnell, of giving the counselee a short scriptural text at the conclusion of the session. Bonnell's rationale for this procedure was twofold. People are most likely to find personal meaning in a brief passage that they can repeat over and over again, and a passage of this nature can break up destructive mental and physical habit patterns and make a "new perspective" possible. But Hiltner sees dangers in this use of Bible verses: "The temptation to use them to induce the feelings we think people ought to have, whether they want such feelings or convictions or not, may be very strong. And over and above that, the reactions people have to the text idea differ very considerably. If given to a person who scorns this idea but is too polite to say so, the likelihood is that the counseling situation has not produced an understanding relationship, and the text will accentuate this rather than make up for it." He concludes that this method can be valuable, but only if "properly and sparingly used."

In concluding his discussion of the Bible as a "resource" in pastoral counseling, Hiltner says that a good biblical scholar should write a book on the subject. In his view, previous books by Dicks, Bonnell, and others treat the issue in a brief, general, and largely anecdotal manner. While not a professional biblical scholar, Wayne E. Oates sought to meet this need for a more systematic treatment of the issue in his book *The Bible in Pastoral Care,* published in 1953.[5] Like Hiltner, Oates is concerned about the misuse of the Bible in pastoral work. He criticizes the pastor who uses it as a symbol of authority, citing the case of a minister who advised a man with homosexual thoughts and habits to place a Bible under his pillow at night "to drive away your evil thoughts and dreams." He also warns against encouraging worship of the Bible, as though it were a good luck charm, and against fostering its ritualistic use, as when "daily Bible-reading" becomes an obsession rather than a search for meaning, direction, and purpose.

Oates points out that these particular misuses of the Bible are common among the mentally ill, which leads him to propose the diagnostic use of the Bible in pastoral care: "The Bible is the pastor's 'royal road' to the deeper levels of the personalities of his people, and particularly to those who are deeply disturbed. Traditionally, the Bible has been used by ministers as a means of reassurance and comfort to people whom they visit and who come to them for counseling help. . . . The use of the Bible as an instrument of diagnosis, however, needs initial attention and extended study."

To illustrate this diagnostic use of the Bible, Oates cites three clinical examples. A twenty-four-year-old woman thought of herself as the wicked servant in the parable of the Talents. The "master" in this case is her husband and the problem is her inability to "submit" to him sexually: "I have taken my gifts and buried them." Another woman reported that she especially loved the biblical story of Jacob, Rachel, and Leah. It turned out that she and her sister had loved the same man, but her sister married him. She then went to live with her sister and her husband, and her hospitalization began when her sister's marriage ended in divorce. The third case involved a twenty-five-year-old woman who was hospitalized when she attempted to kill her five-year-old daughter with a pair of scissors. Earlier that evening her minister had preached on Abraham's sacrifice of Isaac, and she felt "called of the Lord to sacrifice the child." The daughter had been born out of wedlock. This caused the woman's father to disown her, while her daughter became the center of her husband's attention, causing the woman to feel completely isolated.

For Oates, these three cases illustrate "the integral relationship between the dynamic causes of the patients' illness and the use that they make of Biblical material." He notes, however, that these persons are acutely disturbed; less disturbed persons would probably not make such a "bold connection" between their problem and biblical material. He also observes that biblical diagnosis needs to be done with sensitivity. Challenging these patients' interpretations of biblical stories will only serve to "seal off insight and lucid religious thinking, rather than to convince them." But their interpretations of the story are also symptomatic of their illness, so there is a need for "further exploration of the use of the Bible in re-education of a disturbed person." Thus, Oates stresses the need to replace a legalistic approach to the Bible with one that encourages greater sensitivity to one's "inner consciousness of selfhood" and "inner reality of feeling." The psalms encourage such "insight" or "inner revelation," because they express one's "truest and frankest feelings." The reeducation that he has in mind, therefore, is a use of the Bible that encourages the "regular ventilation, catharsis, bringing to light, and resultant insight into one's negative or hostile feelings."

This diagnostic use of the Bible remains a popular idea. In *Psychiatry and Pastoral Care,* published in 1965, Edgar Draper reports on studies at the University of Chicago psychiatric outpatient clinic that used religious data as a diagnostic tool.[6] Psychiatric patients were asked to answer the following questions on the Bible: Who is your favorite Bible character? What is your favorite Bible verse? What is your favorite Bible story? Patients' answers to these questions proved to be most useful in psychiatric diagnosis. A twenty-three-year-old married woman chose Mary Magdalene as her favorite Bible character, noting that most people are unaware that Mary was a prostitute. Her favorite Bible verse was, "Blessed are the pure in heart, for they shall see God," and her favorite Bible story was "Christ being pals with Mary Magdalene."

Oates discusses other uses of the Bible in pastoral work besides the diagnostic one. Another important use is instructional. Sometimes this involves helping parishioners understand the intended meaning of a particular biblical text that they have misunderstood or distorted, such as biblical passages on marriage and divorce. Other times, this means introducing a biblical text or reference that relates to the counselee's problem. A young theological student asks, "Does one have to experience forgiveness through fresh repentance and insight daily?" and Oates responds, "You seem to want to know how the manna is gathered—once and for all, or daily with the dew."

The proverbs and various cryptic sayings attributed to Jesus are especially valuable as instructional devices because "they dart into the mind with the sharpness of a fishhook." Oates recalls the counsel he gave a young father whose wife had just died in childbirth: "Let me help you make the arrangements. Lean on all of us. But remember one thing from God's Word: 'Sufficient unto the day is the evil thereof.'" Months later, the young man reported to Oates that this biblical saying had come to mind again and again as he struggled with new situations brought on by the loss of his wife. Oates believes that Jesus' parables are especially good for instructional purposes. When Jesus was confronted with one of the thorniest of family counseling problems—the conflict of two brothers over the division of a family fortune—Jesus told the parable of the Rich Fool, thereby drawing attention to the problem of covetousness. In deflecting the man's request that he bid his brother divide the inheritance with him, Jesus refused the role of a judge and redefined himself as a moral teacher. Thus, the parable is a particularly effective form of instruction. It challenges counselees to view their current problem in the light of their "long-range intentions," and it enables the counselor to deflect the counselee's attempt to put him in the position of problem solver.

A third important use of the Bible is to bring hope-giving comfort to counselees who are either going through typical crises of life or are having to adjust to bereavement, divorce, chronic illness, or physical handicaps. Here Oates empha-sizes the importance of precision in the selection of biblical passages, and provides examples of readings (many chosen from the psalms) that are appropriate for comforting the frustrated, the disillusioned, the conscience-stricken, and the fearful. He also advocates a deliberate, suggestive, persuasive repetition of the passage to the person in need: "The objective of this is to imbed the idea and thought of the passage just below the conscious level of the person's awareness in such a way that it will be unforgettable, and keep coming back like a song."

Diagnosis, instruction, and *comfort* are just three of the many uses of the Bible in counseling. But Oates gives special attention to these three, noting both their positive uses and their potential dangers. Indiscriminate use of the Bible in pastoral care will do more harm than good. The pastor's use of the Bible should be appropriate to the problem at hand and well timed to the counselee's particular moment of need. The pastor must resist the temptation to offer "many words" of Scripture instead of the "right" or "seasonable" word. On the other hand, one should not be reluctant to let the Bible permeate one's conversation. In fact, the "pastor's own stream of speech, particularly in relation to people who love the Bible, should be filled with the literary smoothness and eloquence of the Bible. . . . Today the pastor who is trained in counseling is prone to use psychological 'jargon' in his speech. He often fails to communicate his real meaning with these relatively obscure and popularly misleading terms. . . . For instance, a more adequate word for 'ambivalence' is 'double-mindedness'; the most graphic expression of 'projec-tion' is the Biblical word 'scapegoat.' Further, the pastor who, by second nature, chooses the Biblical symbol is more

likely to be thought of as a 'shepherd' than as a 'counselor.' "
Thus, while one should use precision when applying the Bible
to a counselee's problems, this should not deter the pastor
from speaking in a biblical mode when that language comes
naturally.

In the conclusion to his book, Oates observes that "a more
profound confrontation of the problems I have raised is in
order." A book that might qualify as this "more profound
confrontation" is Carroll A. Wise's *Psychiatry and the Bible,*
published in 1956, three years after Oates's book.[7] The main
concern of this book is to illuminate biblical understandings
of mental health and illness. In his chapter on fear, anxiety,
and faith, Wise cites the case of a parishioner who came to
his pastor because he was worried about his job, finances, the
children, but mostly about his wife. During counseling, it
came to light that there was a time when he had felt very
resentful toward his wife. Later he had some fears about his
resentment, wondering if it might get out of hand to the point
where he would actually harm her. As time went on, his
resentment lessened, but it was replaced by worry that something might happen to her.

Wise says that this counselee was experiencing anxiety, "a
panic reaction to something that does not constitute an actual
danger to our life, but does constitute a danger to our inner
being, to our self. In John's case anxiety was a symptom of
the deeper problem of resentment." Then, noting that anxiety
may well be "our most pressing problem today," Wise suggests turning to the Bible for insights into the nature of
anxiety. The Bible makes numerous references to anxiety:
"Do not be anxious about your life"; "Have no anxiety about
anything." For some, these passages strengthen the trusting
elements of their personalities and genuinely help them master their anxiety. But for others these passages are less than
helpful. An individual may learn "to say certain passages
that suggest faith over and over to himself. When he has these

passages in his attention, and perhaps for a period afterward, he does not feel anxiety. But he has to repeat this process, and he may find his anxieties returning at times in such force that they completely push all thoughts of faith and trust in God out of his mind." Wise criticizes this process of "repressive self-suggestion . . . because it does not lead us to face and resolve those anxieties which can be resolved or to live with those which cannot."

In Wise's view, there is a better way for the anxious person to appropriate biblical insights. Instead of using biblical statements as aids in repressing feelings of anxiety, we should view the Bible as an account of spiritual struggles similar to our own: "It is because the experiences portrayed in the Bible are similar to our own experiences that we can identify ourselves with its characters." The Bible tells us how other people were confronted with various aspects of anxiety: For Eve, anxiety accompanied temptation. For Esau, it gave rise to the demand for immediate gratification of his need. For Martha, it was the effect of her attempt to bolster relationships by activity. In her case, Jesus "did not give Martha four easy steps to overcome her anxiety; he suggested a deeper and more fundamental approach. The 'good portion' to which Jesus refers is the acceptance of the relationship which Jesus was offering her and which she was avoiding through her own concern with activity."

Thus, the Bible's profound insight into the problem of anxiety is that the key to overcoming anxiety is relationship. Wise points out: "Jesus did not advise—'don't be anxious'— and stop there. As is clear in other passages, he knew that with certain orientations, or certain relationships, people would be anxious. He understood that under some circumstances everyone would feel anxious. But he also knew a different experience, one which realized God as utterly dependable and reliable, so that a man could make a positive response enabling him also to become dependable and reliable." Thus, the Bible diagnoses anxiety as due to disturbed relationships, either between individuals or between the self and God, and it uses stories of various biblical figures to instruct us on this point.

Anxiety is just one theme in Wise's use of the Bible for diagnosis and instruction. Other prominent themes include guilt and forgiveness, and love and hate. But, in every case, Wise emphasizes that the Bible does not advocate repressing negative feelings. On the contrary, expressing feelings such as anger and resentment is a necessary step toward the restoration of relationships, and thus an essential step in the process of regaining mental and spiritual health.

Oates's *The Bible in Pastoral Care* and Wise's *Psychiatry and the Bible* reflect an era in pastoral psychology when there was a strong interest in the use of the Bible in pastoral care and counseling. In the decade that followed the publication of these two books, there were few significant new developments. Various authors offer valuable practical insights, but there are no new methodological advances comparable to Oates's differentiation of the diagnostic, instructional, and comforting uses of the Bible in care and counseling, or Wise's use of the Bible to shed light on the dynamics of psychological illness. This period of calm after considerable activity has been explained in a variety of ways, including the argument that the Rogerian counseling of the day was inhospitable to biblically informed counseling. But another, more important reason is that considerable consensus had been reached about the Bible's role in pastoral counseling. While there are different emphases in Hiltner, Oates, and Wise, they all agree that the Bible can be a valuable resource in pastoral counseling as an aid to exploring the counselee's inner dynamics. Once this consensus on a dynamic understanding of the Bible's role in pastoral counseling was reached, the following decade saw few attempts to challenge or alter this view.

EUROPEAN INTERLUDE

While there were few if any new American contributions during the early 1960s, the issue of the Bible's role in pastoral counseling was kept alive through translations of European works. In 1965, Heije Faber and Ebel van der Schoot devoted a chapter of their book, *The Art of Pastoral Conversation,* to the "distinctive resources in pastoral conversation."[8] In a section of this chapter entitled "The Bible and Other Literature," they discuss the value of pastor-initiated Bible-reading. They make the observation that the reading of the Bible can significantly alter the relationship between pastor and parishioner: "During the conversation there was a certain asymmetry between the partners: on the one hand there was the parishioner who came to the pastor; on the other hand, there was the pastor who gave the parishioner his time. The moment the Bible is read a certain change will take place. Even though the pastor reads, he and the parishioner are in a very similar position, because both of them are addressed by the same word of the Lord." Thus, through Bible-reading, attention shifts from the authority of the pastor to the authority of the word of God.

On the other hand, the authors warn against appealing to the formal authority of the Bible. Since its formal authority has lost much of its value for people today, its authoritativeness will depend on the appropriateness of the selected passage. The pastor should not make overt claims for the Bible's authority. Simply read it, and "the other person will discover what power these words have for him." They also note that Bible-reading often introduces a healthy element of surprise into a pastoral conversation because most parishioners do not expect it. This observation, together with their point that the Bible has lost much of its formal authority, reflects a growing impression among pastoral psychologists that many parishioners are less Bible-oriented than in the past.

Eduard Thurneysen's book *A Theology of Pastoral Care,* which appeared in English translation in 1962, emphasized the importance of the Word of God for pastoral counseling.[9] Thurneysen views pastoral counseling as "a conversation that proceeds from the Word of God and leads to the Word of God. . . . Such conversation does not primarily deal with the presentation of the content of this Word." Thus, what makes the conversation pastoral is not its biblical content, but the fact that the counselee is confronted with the questions that the Word of God puts to him. As Thurneysen puts it: "Pastoral conversation is concerned with the raising and answering of such questions. This defines its form. Life, so to speak, bursts open in these conversations—life in all its dimensions, yet life in confrontation with the proclaimed Word."

While the Bible need not be quoted or read in the pastoral conversation, it provides paradigms of such conversations in the stories of David and the prophet Nathan (I Samuel 11) and Jesus and the Samaritan woman at Jacob's Well (John 4). Thurneysen notes that both conversations concerned cases of adultery, and in both, the counselor's purpose was the disclosure of sin and forgiveness. David's life would have been "irremediably lost, meaningless, and dark if the pastoral conversation had not taken place and set before his eyes what he already basically knew, but only now got to know concretely—that everything depends on forgiveness." In a similar way, Jesus' conversation with the woman at the well revealed the incarnate Word of God, "disclosing and forgiving sin." The "primary event" in these pastoral conversations "is the Word of God itself, which, in and with these conversations, emerges and shows its might over all obscure human affairs." The issue, then, is not whether the Bible is directly quoted, but whether there is disclosure of the forgiveness of sin. In Thurneysen's view, this disclosure is profoundly consoling because it restores the counselee to peace with God. The pastoral conversation is "concerned with the distribution of the treasure of this peace given through the Word of God. Pastoral care means and primarily functions as *care about such peace.* Its practice consists in man's being regarded and addressed in the pastoral conversation as one on whom God in Jesus Christ has laid his mighty and merciful hand."

Besides providing counseling paradigms, certain biblical passages (Matt. 18:12–35; Romans 7 and 8; and Ps. 51) ought to be before the pastor's eyes when the counseling session reaches the point of the disclosure of forgiveness. Thurneysen cites numerous passages in the Psalms, in prophetic writings, in the Gospels, and in the Pauline epistles where forgiveness ends conflict over sin and brings peace. These passages will inform the counselor's handling of the conversation, but they need not be actually quoted or read to the counselee. With Thurneysen's strong emphasis on the Word of God and *its* disclosure in the pastoral conversation, the idea that the Bible is a "resource" that one might use in counseling is almost irrelevant to him. Biblical passages inform the counselor's approach, but disclosure of the Word of God and reading a passage from the Bible are two very different things.

Thurneysen's views have been criticized in this country because he insists that pastoral counseling requires explicit disclosure of the Word of God. Thomas C. Oden and others have argued that God's forgiveness can be communicated implicitly through the concrete counseling relationship, whether or not it is made verbally explicit.[10] These disputes, while theologically important, have tended to obscure the fact that both Thurneysen and his American critics have had less to say about the Bible as a resource in pastoral counseling than the major writers of the previous decade. The mid-1960s ushered in a period in which reference to the Bible was noticeably absent. For instance, Howard J. Clinebell Jr.'s

Basic Types of Pastoral Counseling, the major textbook on pastoral counseling published during the late 1960s, has no sustained discussion of the Bible's role in pastoral counseling.[11]

CONSERVATIVE DEVELOPMENTS

Claiming that theological moderates and liberals were neglecting the Bible's role in pastoral counseling, a number of theologically conservative authors got hold of the issue in the early 1970s. Some of these conservative authors took essentially the same approach as the major authors of the 1950s. An example is Gary Collins' book *Effective Counseling,* published in 1972.[12]

Collins' discussion of the use of "spiritual resources" in counseling takes a middle position between those who contend that reading the Bible or saying a prayer is all that is needed for successful pastoral counseling and those who ignore these spiritual resources in their counseling, using psychological techniques almost exclusively. He favors the use of the Bible in counseling, but says that "no hard and fast rules" can be given for its use: "The extent to which spiritual resources will be used in counseling depends on the counselor, the counselee, and the problem. . . . For some counselees, prayer and Scripture reading during an interview will be a strengthening and reassuring experience. For others, this would be a source of considerable embarrassment and discomfort. Therefore, the counselor must use careful judgment in deciding if, when, and how he introduces such practices." Often, the nature of the problem will be the determining factor. The grief-stricken widow may be greatly comforted by such spiritual resources, whereas a college student who is in danger of flunking out of school may profit more from a long discussion of his study habits. Collins' major concern here is that the Bible not be used indiscriminately. To aid more discriminate use of the Bible in counseling, he provides a chart which recommends Bible passages for thirty different needs and problems.

In the same year that Collins' book appeared (1972), Jay E. Adams' book *Competent to Counsel,* a vigorous argument for "biblical" counseling, was published. Five years later, his book *The Use of the Scriptures in Counseling* appeared.[13] In the later book, Adams lays out the basic tenets of the scriptural counseling approach that he had first advocated in *Competent to Counsel.* These tenets include the following: Scriptural counseling is (1) motivated by the Scriptures; (2) founded propositionally on the Scriptures; (3) structured by the goals and objectives of the Scriptures; and (4) developed systematically in terms of the practices and principles modeled and enjoined in the Scriptures.

For Adams, a major implication of these tenets is that modern psychological theories are totally rejected: "The Christian counselor uses the Scriptures as the sole guide for both counselor and counselee. He rejects eclecticism. He refuses to mix man's ideas with God's. Like every faithful preacher of the Word, he acknowledges the Scripture to be the only source of divine authority and, therefore, judges all other matters by the teaching of the Scriptures." Adams points out that Freudians and Rogerians treat their counselees on the basis of their own presuppositions and do not succumb to an eclectic borrowing of ideas from other theories, so why should the Christian counselor be any less determined to counsel on the basis of biblical presuppositions and these only? He also notes that theological moderates say that psychological theories are not meant to displace the Bible from its central position in pastoral counseling but merely supplement it. But he contends that the Scriptures are all that one needs to counsel, for every conceivable view of human life "is invariably dealt with somewhere or other in the Scriptures." What this means for the Christian counselor is quite clear: "If a principle is new to or different from those that are advocated in the Scriptures, it is wrong; if it is not, it is unnecessary."

Adams illustrates this argument with three cases: a grief-stricken widow, a couple having severe marital conflicts, and a young man whose behavior was so bizarre that he was sent to two different mental hospitals and given a series of shock treatments. Contending that the psychiatrist and clinical psychologist are incompent to handle the first case of bereavement, Adams says that the Christian counselor knows that he is up to the task because he is "armed with God's scriptural promises": "You know that among God's children, you *can* (as Paul put it) 'comfort one another' with God's words (I Thessalonians 4:18); you know that God has said that the Scriptural data in I Thessalonians 4 will act as an anchor for the believer to keep his grief from drifting into despair, and that they will moderate that grief by balancing it with hope so that in the end, through scriptural counsel the widow is enabled to sorrow in the way different from others 'who have no hope' (I Thessalonians 4:13)." Thus, the Christian counselor, armed with God's scriptural promises, is able to engage in "in-depth" grief counseling.

In the second case, that of the couple with seemingly irreconcilable differences, Adams again points out that the scriptural counselor has all that is needed to meet the situation adequately. The counselor says to the couple: "Since the information that you have given me indicates that you have no scriptural warrant for dissolving this marriage, there is but one course open to you: repentance and reconciliation followed by the building of an entirely new relationship that is pleasing to God." The counselor then informs the couple that the Bible contains all the information they will need to make these changes, citing some of the "many hopeful biblical specifics about such change," and concludes: "If you mean business with God, even though your marriage presently is in a desperate condition, within a few weeks you can have instead a marriage that sings! Indeed, there is no reason why the first steps toward God's dramatic change cannot be taken *this* week, beginning *today.* What do you say?" Adams explains that the counselor is being authoritative and directive here because, apart from such authoritative direction, all is in flux, nothing is certain, and there is no foundation for hope: "Every directive of God—no matter how far short of it that we may come at the moment—serves to provide a solid foundation for the Christian's hope. Both counselor and counselee, therefore, may take heart in scriptural counseling for the very reason that it is authoritative."

In the third case, that of the young man who exhibited bizarre behavior, the counselor assumed that sin was at the root of the problem. He did so on the grounds that the Bible considers all nonorganic causes of bizarre behavior to be due to the sin of the individual. Since organic causes could be ruled out in this case, sin was the only explanation the Bible would support. The next task was to identify the sin that was causing this strange behavior. After a few counseling sessions, the counselor discovered that the counselee "had been sinning against his body" by failing to get adequate sleep. His bizarre behavior always followed periods of sleep loss. He "was convicted of his sin against God and, following forgiveness, was placed on a carefully monitored sleep regimen, his daily schedule was revised to biblical life priorities, and the problem was erased."

Interestingly enough, these three cases illustrate Oates's three uses of the Bible in counseling. The first shows how the Bible comforts, the second how it instructs, and the third how it diagnoses. But, apart from this similarity between Adams and Oates, the authors of the 1950s have little in common with Adams. In the first place, Adams does not believe that a Christian counselor can ever choose *not* to apply the Bible to the counselee's problem. He would not agree with their view (or that of Gary Collins) that use of the Bible in the counseling session may depend on the circumstances involved. To him, there is no possible circumstance for which the Bible would not be appropriate.

In the second place, the previous authors were concerned that the selected Bible passage might not fit the counselee's situation. Adams only worries that the counselor will misunderstand the basic intention of a passage: "The counselor must know the *purpose* of the passage; that is, he must know what God intended to do to the reader (warn, encourage, motivate, etc.) with those words. Then, he must make God's purpose his own in the application of the passage to human needs." This is done by attending to cues in the passage itself. For example, the statement in John's Gospel that it was written "that you may believe."

In the third place, in contrast to the previous authors, Adams believes that modern psychotherapeutic theory and practice are incompatible with the Christian faith and distract the counselor from biblical insights. He cites the example of a young couple who came to their pastor for help in disciplining their seven-year-old son. Adams claims that a minister steeped in modern psychotherapeutic thinking would consider spanking to be a last resort after all other methods had failed. But the minister who is grounded in the Bible knows that spanking is exactly what is needed because Prov. 22:15 says, "Folly is bound up in the heart of a child, but the rod of discipline drives it far from him." Spanking, then, is not a last resort, it is "a vital biblical disciplinary method." On the other hand, this minister will also know that spanking is not enough, for Prov. 29:15 says that "the rod and *reproof* give wisdom." The minister will therefore instruct the parents that the child, besides being given corporal punishment, must be confronted with his sin and need for redemptive change. In this illustration of the dangers of modern psychotherapeutic theory, Adams is being critical of another conservative author, Bruce Narramore, who says that parents should take to heart Prov. 23:7, "As a man thinketh in his heart, so is he," and on this basis carefully instruct their children about the reasons for the family rules so that correct behavior may follow from a proper understanding of them. Adams says that it "does not take a prophet to predict the consequences of such an approach," and accuses Narramore of being influenced by "modified Rogerianistic behaviorism."

MODERATE RESURGENCE

Conservative discussions of the Bible's role in pastoral counseling were dominant in the 1970s. But there were signs by the late 1970s that theological moderates and liberals were taking renewed interest in the topic. John B. Cobb, Jr., signaled this revival in *Theology and Pastoral Care,* published in 1977.[14] He contends that "the time may have come for us to bring our language-world and that of the Bible together, while allowing the Biblical language to retain its own meaning." Should this happen, "pastoral counselors could experience their counseling not simply as in continuity with Christianity in its ultimate purposes but as informed by the Christian heritage in both form and substance."

Like authors in the 1950s, Cobb worries that recovery of biblical language in pastoral counseling could lead to its indiscriminate use. But, more than they, he is concerned about the possible irrelevancy of the Bible. If used, "it must grow out of the living experience of Christian people who are fully immersed in the modern world. They must find that the authentic use of biblical language illumines their experience and brings to consciousness aspects of that experience that have been neglected or obscured by modern conceptualities. . . . If this occurs, and only when it occurs, will it become proper and natural to employ such language in pastoral counseling."

Cobb makes this suggestion for the recovery of biblical language toward the end of his book, and does not have much more to say about how this might look in practice. However, the issue of the Bible in pastoral counseling was taken up the following year by David Switzer in *Pastor, Preacher, Person.* [15] Switzer takes the view, stressed earlier by Hiltner, that any use of the Bible should not violate basic counseling principles. Following the research of Robert H. Carkhuff, he points out that effective counseling requires accurate empathy, respect for the counselee, concreteness, genuineness, self-disclosure by the counselor, confrontation, and immediacy. Thus, any use of the Bible in pastoral counseling should be consistent with these conditions of effective counseling.

Switzer also takes up the view, emphasized by Oates, that the counselor's role sometimes involves biblical reeducation. He cites the case of a counselee who refused to consider his wife's desire to work outside the home, using "wives, be subject to your husbands" (Eph. 5:22) to justify this refusal. The pastor showed the counselee that this verse needs to be viewed in relation to its location within a larger discussion of reciprocity in marriage. Thus, the counselee was educated in the Bible, his attitude toward his wife shown to be incongruent with the spirit of the Christian gospel. Switzer recommends a similar approach in the case of a divorcee who felt guilty because she divorced her husband for reasons other than adultery (Matt. 5:32).

Switzer also emphasizes the diagnostic use of the Bible in counseling. He discusses the case of a young married man who became emotionally distraught and began to identify with Daniel in the lions' den. It was clear to the counselor that the young man chose this story because he felt trapped, with no realistic hope of escape.

Thus, Switzer's chapter on the Bible reflects many of the same interests and emphases of the consensus reached in the late 1950s. His book marks the resurgence of the view that the Bible can be an important resource in pastoral counseling if used in a discriminating and sensitive way.

A third and particularly important author in this period of moderate resurgence is William B. Oglesby, Jr. His *Biblical Themes for Pastoral Care,* published in 1980, is the only book devoted solely to the Bible in pastoral counseling during this period.[16] His approach in this book is based, in part, on his earlier article, "Pastoral Care and Counseling in Biblical Perspective," published in 1973.[17] In this article, he discussed three types of psychotherapies, those that give primacy to *knowing,* to *doing,* and to *being.* Psychoanalysis and Eric Berne's transactional analysis are *knowing* therapies, William Glasser's reality therapy is a *doing* therapy, and Carl Rogers' client-centered therapy and Fritz Perls's Gestalt therapy are *being* therapies. Oglesby argues that the Bible affirms all three objectives, but *being* is given primacy in its scale of values, and *knowing* and *doing* are derivative of *being.* From this analysis, Oglesby concludes that "those forms of therapy which move toward *being* are more consistent with the biblical point of view than those which move toward *knowing* or *doing.* " This, says Oglesby, is the essence of Thomas Oden's argument in *Kerygma and Counseling* (1966) that Carl·Rogers' counseling theory is "an operational demonstration of the unconditional divine love which is the heart of the gospel."

Oglesby's article on pastoral counseling in biblical perspective is significant in two important respects. In the first place, it brings the biblical perspective to bear on the *process* of counseling—its methods, its objectives, and its understanding of the counselor-counselee relationship. He contends that books on the subject of the Bible in pastoral care and counseling fall into two broad categories, those which "tend to deal with the understanding of the human situation gained from a biblical point of view" and those which discuss "the way the Bible may be used in the pastoral work of the minister."

Regarding the two major books written in the 1950s, Wise's book reflects the former approach, while Oates's reflects the latter. In Oglesby's view, neither approach deals "specifically with the sense in which biblical material informs process."

In the second place, Oglesby views the Bible as a document that has a theological unity running through its "varieties of forms," a unity based on the primacy it gives to *being*. This unity reflects the Bible's view that "the essential problem of man is not that he is ignorant and thus needs to be taught, although knowledge is never taken lightly; nor is the difficulty that he is an evil-doer who must be pressed for right behavior, although good works are never ignored; rather his problem is that he is a sinner who needs forgiveness and reconciliation, from which come both right *knowing* and right *doing.*"

This emphasis on the theological unity of the Bible raises a problem that Oglesby does not discuss in his 1973 article but takes up in his book. This concerns the fact that, while man's basic problem is that he is a sinner in need of forgiveness and reconciliation, the Bible deals with this problem in a variety of ways. Oglesby attempts to take account of this variety by employing a thematic approach. He says that "the biblical perspective" has a central theme, that man's central problem is that he is a sinner who needs forgiveness and reconciliation, and that God is acting for and with mankind toward reconciliation and restoration. But this central theme is reflected in various subthemes, including *initiative and freedom, fear and faith, conformity and rebellion, death and rebirth,* and *risk and redemption.* Thus, the basic theme enables us to examine the various biblical texts "and so determine their meaning for the work of ministry. However, the task is facilitated by attention to the subthemes that are woven into this basic strand and that recur over and again in first one setting and then another."

Oglesby shows how each subtheme sheds light on the basic

theme, and explains how this subtheme may function in the counseling process itself. For example, in his discussion of the subtheme of fear and faith, Oglesby uses various biblical examples of fear to show that fear "always gives rise to hiding, to a distortion of reality, to a frantic effort toward some sort of defense or protection," and faith overcomes fear when the fearful are assured that God's love reaches them even in their places of hiding and defense. He illustrates this fear/faith dynamic with a counseling case in which the counselee was able to explore "aspects of himself long submerged under the deadly shell of hiding." Thus, Oglesby's use of subthemes enables him to show that the biblical perspective, while reflecting a basic unifying theme, deals with the complexity of problems that arise in pastoral care and counseling. These subthemes serve much the same purpose that Paul W. Pruyser claimed for his theological themes (providence,. repentance, faith, grace, vocation, communion, and awareness of the holy) in *The Minister as Diagnostician,* that they "linger in the pastor's mind, functioning as guideposts to his diagnostic thinking and as ordering principles for the observations he makes."[18]

In developing this thematic understanding of the Bible, Oglesby acknowledges his debt to Gerhard von Rad, Martin Noth, and Walther Eichrodt, the Old Testament scholars who sought to identify the major themes in the historical books of the Old Testament. Oglesby contends that his subthemes are based on the Yahwist material, beginning with the primeval history and moving through the patriarchal history, and thus rooted in the "basic thrust of the Bible." His use of modern biblical scholarship is a unique feature of Oglesby's book. None of the previous authors made significant use of this scholarly work. He deserves credit for using modern biblical scholarship in developing his thematic approach.

On the other hand, I would like to point out a weakness in his use of biblical scholarship, because it bears directly on the approach that I am developing here. This is his tendency to ignore the fact that the Bible consists of different oral forms and literary genres which influence the way its themes are represented. For example, in his discussion of the sub-theme of fear and faith, Oglesby says: "From Genesis to Revelation, the reply to Adam's terror and Cain's anguished cry is the same, 'You don't have to be afraid.' Thus, the theme of fear takes various forms in the Bible, but the purpose is always the same, i.e. to retreat behind a facade, to put on a mask, to erect some sort of wall or barrier, to banish or destroy, anything to find protection from a relationship that protends destruction." There may be some truth in the claim that the purpose of fear is always the same, wherever it occurs in the Bible, but the meaning that it has in any given biblical text is inseparable from the oral form or literary genre in which this fear is recounted, whether a *legendary* account of Cain's fear of being slain, a *gospel* account of the disciples' fear of following Jesus, or an *apocalyptic* account of the fearful anticipation of the Son of Man's appearance.

The importance of the oral form in determining the meaning of a biblical theme is reflected in the Yahwist material which provides the basis for Oglesby's own subthemes. As Old Testament scholar Claus Westermann points out, the stories in Genesis are not hero sagas in the traditional sense but "family narratives." These stories are concerned with various family relationships, including parent-child relationships in the Abraham cycle, brother relationships in the Jacob-Esau cycle, and the intertwining of parent-child and brother relationships in the Joseph cycle.[19] Whether these cycles of stories are viewed as hero sagas or as family narratives will make considerable difference in how we understand their themes. Moreover, we can readily see how Oglesby's themes derive from the oral forms in which the Genesis materials were originally cast. His themes of *initiative and freedom, fear and faith,* and *conformity and rebellion* grow out of the family narrative form, but his themes of *death and rebirth* and *risk and redemption* do not. These two themes have their basis in the stories in Genesis 1–11 which, in Westermann's view, are not family narratives but narratives reflecting a more universal scope and centered on issues of guilt and punishment. Thus, specific biblical themes emerge from specific kinds of forms. And, while themes like fear and faith may appear in various places in the Bible, both Old and New Testament, their meanings are inseparable from the oral forms and the literary genres in which they occur. This means that we should be especially attentive to these forms and genres when relating the Bible to pastoral counseling.

WHERE DO WE GO FROM HERE?

To set the stage for my own approach, I want to summarize what we have learned from the literature just surveyed, because the practical and theoretical insights of this literature, especially during the "emerging consensus" and "moderate resurgence" periods, serve as the foundation for this approach. What theoretical and practical insights do these books and articles offer? What does this literature tell us about the potential role of the Bible in pastoral counseling?

First, there is broad agreement among these authors, especially during the "emerging consensus" and "moderate resurgence" periods, that any use of the Bible in pastoral counseling should be done with discrimination. The early authors were especially concerned about the possible misuse of the Bible in counseling. To avoid this, Dicks recommended approaching the use of the Bible from the perspective of the specific needs of the counselee. One should discover what these needs are and then select the Bible passage relevant to them. For Dicks, the needs that the Bible is best able to address are needs of the spirit (confidence, endurance, peace, release from worry, and so forth). These are perennial needs of human beings, and many passages of the Bible are addressed to these needs. Hiltner suggests that the counselor be especially attentive to how the counselee will perceive references to the Bible. Will this be perceived as a distraction? as an exercise of pastoral authority? The pastor who fails to take the counselee's perceptions and feelings into account is likely to find that his use of the Bible in counseling is counterproductive, that it actually impedes the counseling process.

Thus, there is general agreement that any use of the Bible in counseling should not violate the principles on which the counselor normally operates. The Bible should not be introduced into the pastoral conversation if this means that the methods and goals of the counseling session are thereby abrogated. Hiltner warns that when the Bible is introduced, this often changes the whole tone of the counseling session, especially the relationship between the counselor and the counselee. Instead of furthering the goals of understanding and acceptance, it may create a barrier between them, and distract them from the issues that need to be addressed if the counselee is to be helped. On the other hand, Faber and van der Schoot suggest that, sometimes, Bible-reading in pastoral conversation can help to establish the desired relationship between the pastor and the counselee. Instead of setting the pastor and the counselee apart, driving a wedge between them, Bible-reading can actually put them on the same level —two people addressed by the word of God—and thus contribute to mutual trust and understanding.

Second, there is general agreement among these authors that the Bible has a number of different uses in counseling, that the Bible can be used to comfort, to instruct, and to diagnose. This means that it is important for the pastor to have a clear understanding of what particular purpose the Bible serves in any given case. Because he worked mainly with hospital patients, Dicks almost invariably employs the Bible for the purpose of giving comfort. On the other hand,

Draper, a psychiatrist, focuses almost exclusively on the diagnostic use of the Bible, and Switzer, who has involvement in both seminary education and psychiatric settings, focuses on the educational and diagnostic uses of the Bible. Thus, it appears that how one uses the Bible in counseling is partly determined by the setting in which one ministers. Still, it should be emphasized that the Bible can be put to various kinds of uses, each having its unique therapeutic value. Pastors who have used the Bible as a book of comfort discover new ways of employing the Bible in their pastoral work as they explore its diagnostic and instructional uses.

To authors like Oates and Draper, the Bible can be used diagnostically, because many Christians identify with biblical characters. Some feel perpetually homeless in the world, like Abraham. Others always seem to disappoint their Lord at the most inopportune times, like Peter. Still others are inwardly divided between the composed Mary and the responsible Martha. While there is the danger that the diagnostic use of the Bible in counseling will be thought of as merely a clinical tool, diagnosis can mean using biblical insights to gain a more empathetic understanding of the counselee's struggles and conflicts. It can also mean evaluating the counselee's current difficulties from the perspective of biblical accounts of God's healing activity. In my judgment, Jesus' parabolic vision is a particularly valuable biblical resource for this purpose.

To authors like Switzer, the educational use of the Bible in counseling has particular value in cases where the counselee is misusing a biblical reference to legitimate behavior or attitudes that are inconsistent with the basic thrust of the Christian gospel. As Switzer shows, the pastor's educational task may involve helping the counselee to acquire a more adequate understanding of what a biblical passage means and how it can be more responsibly applied to the situation in question. Most of the authors who deal with this educational use of the Bible focus on family problems. Oates takes up the

problem of dividing the family inheritance, Switzer deals
with divorce and husband-wife relationships, and Adams is
especially concerned with the problem of child discipline.
Their examples indicate that many Christians turn to the
Bible for guidance in matters of family conflict, but because
these conflicts have prompted them to focus on particular
passages, they often use these Bible verses in an argumentative or defensive spirit. Switzer shows that the pastoral counseling setting provides an atmosphere in which the counselee
can lower his defenses and explore the passage in a more
constructive, positive way. In this way, the counseling setting
is itself an educational model. When the pastor explores this
biblical passage with the counselee without becoming defensive, argumentative, or authoritarian, he provides a model for
more constructive ways of handling family conflicts.

A third important insight of this literature is the idea that
the Bible may inform the counseling process itself. The earlier authors, such as Hiltner, emphasized that any use of the
Bible should not violate the counseling methods otherwise
employed in the counseling. But Oglesby puts this point in
a much more positive way when he suggests that the Bible
may actually inform the methods, objectives, and counselor-
counselee relationship of the counseling process. He proposes
to do this through the use of biblical themes. My objective
is the same, but I propose to accomplish it through the use
of biblical forms.

An analogy might help to point up the difference in the two
approaches. The counseling process may be compared to a
river flowing into the sea. If we are concerned about the
movement of the water as it flows downstream, thematic
analysis can be exceedingly helpful. But if we are concerned
about the river's direction and ultimate destination, we will
want to attend to formal considerations. In my judgment, we
need to give first priority to the task of analyzing the riverbed
and charting the riverbanks. After this is done, we can take

up the task of identifying and interpreting the themes that flow within these formal boundaries.[20]

The Bible has different ways of addressing our religious needs. Taking biblical forms seriously results in a much more carefully controlled approach than is normally the case. It rejects the random selection of biblical verses out of context which often prevails when pastors try to counsel "biblically."

This more controlled approach to the role of the Bible in pastoral counseling has direct implications for the different uses of the Bible and the importance of using it in a discriminating way. For, in this approach, one must consciously choose a form that harmonizes with the present purpose of counseling, such as comforting, instructing, or diagnosing. Oates suggested that the proverb and the parable may both be used for instructional purposes. But the approach that will be developed here shows that, while a proverb does instruct, the parable has other possibilities. Thus, we cannot assume that any given form will serve any aim of pastoral counseling. This is one place where our use of the Bible in pastoral counseling needs to be more discriminating—not because the counselee may demand it, but because faithfulness to the Bible and its intentions requires such discrimination.

The next step in the "moderate resurgence" is to give serious attention to the role of biblical forms in shaping the pastoral counseling process. I now want to turn to this fundamental task.

Chapter 2
The Use of Psalms
and Grief Counseling

Surely the psalms have been deeply meaningful to many generations of believers. A vast range of emotions can be evoked by such phrases as "The LORD is my shepherd," "O come, let us sing to the LORD," or "My God, why hast thou forsaken me?" Accordingly, pastoral counselors have frequently considered the psalms a valuable resource, although in a variety of ways.

In this chapter, we will first take up the prevailing view in pastoral counseling that the psalms are useful for exploring the counselee's feelings. Second, we will lay the groundwork for a more systematic approach to this view of the psalms by exploring the work of biblical scholars on the psalm of lament. Third, we will develop this approach in detail by showing how the lament may structure the process of grief counseling. The chapter concludes with proposals for the use of selected psalms in grief counseling.

Hiltner, Oates, and Wise discuss many different biblical texts, but they center on the psalms in defining their basic understanding of the Bible's role in pastoral counseling. A major reason for their emphasis on the psalms is the psalms' reflection of human emotional experience, and for these authors, pastoral counseling aims to help counselees express and clarify their feelings. By "feelings," they do not mean emotions that come and go, but deep feelings that reflect serious intrapsychic conflicts. They see in the psalms a similar engagement with such deep conflicting feelings as resentment, anxiety, envy, anger, and despair, on the one hand, and gratitude, serenity, confidence, and joy on the other. Let's take a closer look at how each of these authors appropriates the psalms for pastoral counseling, keeping in mind their common emphasis on the counselee's inner feelings.

THE PSALMS AND EXPLORATION OF INNER FEELINGS

Seward Hiltner and the Case of Psalm 38

Hiltner's discussion of the Bible as a "religious resource" in pastoral counseling focuses on a counseling session in which the counselee introduced Psalm 38.[21] The counselee, Erwin F. Arkwright, was a pillar of the church. His wife had died five years earlier. After his third child married and moved out, he was looked after by a housekeeper. He was in a type of business where the temptations to gouge, within the law, are numerous. He had talked with the pastor privately on many occasions, and felt that Pastor Weems was very helpful to him at the time of his wife's death, so they established good rapport. On this particular evening, Arkwright began by saying that he wanted to talk about Psalm 38: "I read it last night, and I had the most peculiar reaction to it." They decided to read the whole psalm over first.

PSALM 38

1 O LORD, rebuke me not in thy wrath: neither chasten me in thy hot displeasure.

2 For thine arrows stick fast in me, and thy hand presseth me sore.

3 There is no soundness in my flesh because of thine anger; neither is there any rest in my bones because of my sin.

4 For mine iniquities are gone over mine head: as an heavy burden they are too heavy for me.

5 My wounds stink and are corrupt because of my foolishness.

6 I am troubled; I am bowed down greatly; I go mourning all the day long.

7 For my loins are filled with a loathsome disease: and there is no soundness in my flesh.

8 I am feeble and sore broken: I have roared by reason of the disquietness of my heart.

9 Lord, all my desire is before thee; and my groaning is not hid from thee.

10 My heart panteth, my strength faileth me: as for the light of mine eyes, it also is gone from me.

11 My lovers and my friends stand aloof from my sore; and my kinsmen stand afar off.

12 They also that seek after my life lay snares for me: and they that seek my hurt speak mischievous things, and imagine deceits all the day long.

13 But I, as a deaf man, heard not; and I was as a dumb man that openeth not his mouth.

14 Thus I was as a man that heareth not, and in whose mouth are no reproofs.

15 For in thee, O LORD, do I hope: thou wilt hear, O Lord my God.

16 For I said, Hear me, lest otherwise they should rejoice over me: when my foot slippeth, they magnify themselves against me.

17 For I am ready to halt, and my sorrow is continually before me.

18 For I will declare mine iniquity; I will be sorry for my sin.

19 But mine enemies are lively, and they are strong: and they that hate me wrongfully are multiplied.

20 They also that render evil for good are mine adversaries; because I follow the thing that good is.

21 Forsake me not, O LORD: O my God, be not far from me.

22 Make haste to help me, O Lord my salvation.

When the reading was finished, Arkwright said: "There, now you can see what I mean. If I understand the psalmist, he feels the forces of evil are sneaking up close to him." He went on to explain how the psalmist's feelings are "disturbingly how I have been feeling sometimes lately." It's not that "certain people are ganging up on me—I don't have a persecution complex—but it's as if life were ganging up on me." He then alluded to the loss of his wife and his continued loneliness.

But his personal identification with the psalmist did not stop there. He went on to relate his situation to specific statements in the psalm: "When I read about the Lord's arrows sticking fast in me, it touched something; that's the way I felt. I got to feeling worse and worse. And when I got to that place about being feeble, that's exactly how I felt. And then that bit about speaking mischievous things—I got to thinking about business." He began to relate how his business colleagues would laugh at his high moral principles and could not understand why he insisted on maintaining them. Then last night he began to wonder: Do I understand it? What is the use of maintaining these standards? And again he felt like the psalmist, who also wondered why he continued to do the right thing: "We're doing it, but we don't really see much in it." He concluded by asking the pastor if he was reading the psalmist correctly or whether he was reading thoughts into the psalmist's words? Is this what the psalmist really meant?

In response, Pastor Weems noted that the psalmist takes a series of steps as the psalm proceeds: "First he faces the fact of how he feels. He doesn't just say, 'I feel bad, but I know I shouldn't; therefore I don't.' He admits it. He even tells himself that he had tried to overlook the facts for a long time;

he was like a deaf man or a dumb man. He had thought he could get along by being perfect, never letting his foot slip. But that didn't help. So next he realizes there must be something about himself, his own sin. So he tells the Lord he is a sinner. But in the next breath he says his enemies follow evil, while he actually follows good. He asks the Lord not to forsake him. He feels he is a good man, though a sinner, but he still feels alone. What can he do? He doesn't know, except call on God to hurry and help him."

Arkwright agreed that the psalmist takes a regular series of steps, but "he doesn't get anywhere. He may be courageous in admitting how he feels, but what good does it do?" Pastor Weems acknowledged that there "seems to be something missing. . . . And if we could see why he didn't get anywhere, it might have a message for you." With Arkwright's encouragement, Pastor Weems went on to indicate what he felt was missing. In the first place, the psalmist confesses his sin in a very general way. It is good that he confesses his sin, but he fails to make it specific. What was the nature of the sin? He never tells us. In the second place, he turns to the Lord because he does not know what else to do, but he seems to lack confidence that God will help him.

Arkwright responded favorably to this analysis, especially to the idea that the psalmist confesses sin in a general way and fails to get down to specifics. He guessed that his own specific sin was that he had been going to the cemetery too often and shying away from anything but casual friendships. This led Weems to note a third important aspect of the psalmist's failure, the fact that it never occurs to the psalmist that there is any way out except to go it alone. He tells his former friends to stay away and he seems aloof to potential friends. "In other words, he doesn't think that the right road may be through any kind of social channels, association and friendship with other people, but only through isolation and loneliness." Arkwright said he thought there was a "great deal" in what the pastor was saying and indicated that he wanted to think this over a couple of days and then perhaps talk with Weems again. The session ended with both men offering a brief prayer, with Arkwright stressing the theme of understanding the meaning of the Holy Word for our lives.

In analyzing this case, Hiltner points out that the situation was defined from the outset. It was to be an exploration of Psalm 38 "to see if Arkwright's feelings about it throw any light on his feelings about life." Thus, Pastor Weems did not try to tell the counselee that the psalm applied to him in all particulars, but instead attempted to delineate the psalmist's feelings and then leave it to Arkwright to determine which feelings were applicable to him and which were not. Hiltner also suggests that the pastor deserves praise for soft-pedaling the psalmist's "paranoid" feelings, the psalmist's "intense and circular preoccupation with blame." Such feelings were not applicable to Arkwright because he did not have a "persecution complex."

Hiltner's analysis of the case centers on *feelings*. As Hiltner notes, Pastor Weems pointed out that the psalmist "faces the fact of how he feels. He doesn't just say, 'I feel bad, but I know I shouldn't; therefore I don't.' He admits it." Weems applauded this facing up to one's feelings, but was then critical of the psalmist because, while ready "to tell all the different ways in which he feels bad," he does not "seem ready to make any connection between how he feels and what has happened to him and in him to make him feel that way." Thus, the psalmist fails to gain *insight* into the sin that has given rise to these feelings. Arkwright resonated with this analysis of how the psalmist expressed but failed to probe the causes of his feelings when he said that he too had been "feeling sorry for myself" but was not "specific enough" about his sin either. Yet, when he read the psalm, Arkwright felt "moved by it" because he experienced a "companionship of feelings" with the psalmist. He could identify with the psalmist's feelings of loneliness because he had not gotten over the loss of his wife, and with the psalmist's feelings of being the laughingstock of his enemies because he was the object of his business associates' ridicule. Accompanying these specific feelings was an overall, pervasive feeling of futility. He found the psalmist's resigned plea at the end of the psalm—"Forsake me not, O LORD!"—to be rather small consolation, but this too was a feeling he knew and shared with the psalmist.

Thus, if the session helped the counselee, Hiltner indicates that it was primarily in helping him gain insight into his feelings. Most promising in this regard was Arkwright's confession that perhaps he had not been allowing himself to form new relationships, that he had been trying to carry his burden all by himself. His admission that perhaps he was making too many lonely trips to the cemetery and not reaching out enough to others was an important insight. If he was feeling down, he was beginning to realize that this was partly of his own making, and that he should begin to do something about it, like forming new friendships. Thus he gained constructive insight into the causes of his negative feelings. As he left the session, he seemed open to relating more to others. At least, he agreed to think about this and to talk with Pastor Weems about it again if it seemed appropriate. The psalmist's tendency toward "paranoid feelings" served here as a negative example, a catalyst toward a better way of working with their "companionship of feelings" through forming new relationships.

Carroll Wise and the Case of Psalm 38

Like Hiltner, Carroll Wise also focuses on the feeling dimension of the psalms. In Chapter 1 of his book *Psychiatry and the Bible,* he has an important section on "health and illness in the Bible."[22] His analysis of Psalm 38, the same psalm that Hiltner uses, is the cornerstone of this discussion, setting the tone for his biblical understanding of health and illness. In his view, this psalm provides an "interesting study of a poet's interpretation of the relation of his illness to his religious life." The psalmist sees illness as the outgrowth of sin, an insight that "is parallel to the point of view of modern psychosomatic medicine in so far as it finds one of the factors in physical illness to be intense feelings of guilt." Wise emphasizes that *feelings* of guilt are the important factor. Illness can be a punishment inflicted from outside ourselves, but it is also the result of feelings that we experience within. Such "feelings of guilt are subjective, and may be produced in us by conditions that are or are not our responsibility."

Wise stresses that people today can readily relate to the feelings of the psalmist. We can feel the psalmist's "cry of desperation and utter distress," the "sense of agony and helplessness." We can also empathize with the psalmist's conflicting feelings about God. As Wise points out: "In this psalm we are dealing with conflicting feelings about God. On the one side he punishes; on the other, he understands and even participates in suffering. Many people have similar conflicting feelings about God. By facing and examining such feelings we may gain insight into ourselves and into the experiences out of which these feelings grow." The psalm shows that conflicting feelings about God ought not to be repressed. When we acknowledge and examine them, we gain insight into ourselves and the experiences that provoked these feelings. This typically involves the discovery that we have been experiencing severe inner conflict from which we seek relief.

Wise discusses other psalms besides Psalm 38 in his section on health and illness in the Bible, but his analysis of this particular psalm establishes his view that the psalms are relevant to pastoral care because they deal with inner feelings, usually of a deeply conflictful nature. He agrees with Hiltner that, by exploring these feelings, we are able to gain the insight into ourselves that makes positive change possible. But, while both recognize that the psalmist in Psalm 38 expresses deep feelings, they are less certain that the psalmist has gained insight leading to positive change. Hiltner appears to agree with the pastor that the psalmist was not specific enough about what caused these feelings, and he adds that some of the psalmist's feelings were "paranoid" in nature, suggesting that the psalmist wanted to externalize these inner conflicts instead of gaining insight into them. Wise puts it this way: "In Psalm 38 there is an expectation of God's help, but not an expression of achieved cure." This criticism, of course, is leveled at the psalmist and not at the Bible as such. Wise's detailed analyses of biblical understandings of anxiety, guilt, love, and hate show that insight into one's deeper feelings is necessary to positive change. His criticism of the psalmist is based on the fact that the psalmist has not yet acted on this important biblical truth.

Wayne Oates and the Comforting Role of Psalms

For Oates, the psalms are central to the Bible's *comforting* role. He discusses this use of the Bible in his chapter "The Bible as a Book of Comfort."[23] In the opening paragraphs of this chapter, he contends that the Bible does not comfort merely by helping individuals adjust to their plight. Instead, he cites with approval John Sutherland Bonnell's view that the Bible is "a means of stimulating and generating the necessary psychic energy" to enable one to "accept responsibility for doing the thing" that is "necessary and inevitable" for one's own "salvation and healing." In Oates's view, Bonnell used the Bible as "a therapeutic instrument" which enables people to lay hold of "new spiritual energies." This kind of "in-spiriting" ministry has parallels in the "supportive therapy" of secular psychology, but "the obvious examples of the strength imparted to helpless people through the use of the inspirational power of the Scriptures indicate that the so-called insight of the psychotherapeutic interview is cold and dead apart from some revelation of spiritual resources of creative power." Thus, when Oates talks about the Bible's hope-giving comfort, he means its role in bringing new spiritual resources to an individual's awareness.

With this understanding of the comforting role of pastoral counseling, Oates identifies four types of troubled individuals who can profit from the comforting resources of the Bible. These include the *frustrated*, the *disillusioned and embittered*, the *conscience-stricken*, and the *fearful*. He especially recommends the use of selected psalms in dealing with the first two. For those who are frustrated, psalms "are of particular comfort to a person who has experienced the sudden frustration of a deep-seated and long-cherished desire. For instance, the married couple who have discovered that they can never have children or the parents whose child was born dead." When such profound frustration of one's desire gives way to more extreme disillusionment, one needs to "pour out the bitterness in a catharsis of negative feelings." When this happens, "the pendulum tends to swing back and he or she begins to construct more positive feelings and attitudes. This pouring out of feelings needs to come quickly, lest they become rancid and then turn chronic in bitterness." Oates recommends Psalm 23 for comforting those who are frustrated and Psalms 27 and 37 for those who have poured out their bitter feelings.

He emphasizes, however, that the cathartic release of negative feelings is only the first step in a larger therapeutic process that leads from the venting of negative feelings to the emergence of positive feelings. The major purpose of the psalms in this process is to encourage the development of new *positive* feelings to counteract any tendency toward chronic bitterness. Oates does not recommend reading passages from psalms that actually give vent to *negative* feelings, but instead says that the counselee may be receptive to the Scriptures when "the positive feelings begin to emerge." Then, the psalms contribute to the therapeutic process of laying hold of new and positive spiritual energies: "Commit thy way unto the LORD; trust also in him, and he will bring it to pass" (Ps. 37:5). For Oates, this trust is the ultimate source of new positive feelings.

Hiltner, Wise, and Oates all agree that the psalms focus attention on the counselee's inner feelings. All three authors stress the importance of giving vent to one's inner feelings—particularly negative ones—but none stops there. They view this venting of inner feelings as a necessary step toward positive change, first through insight into one's feelings, then through the infusion of new spiritual energies to replace the negative feelings. Each recognizes the psalms' value in assisting this movement toward positive change.

The Shepherding Role of the Psalms

Appreciation for the psalms is also reflected in the emphasis of these authors on the shepherding role of the counselor. As indicated in Chapter 1, Oates advocates the counselor's use of biblical language instead of psychological jargon so that the counselee will view the counselor as a "shepherd."

Hiltner's view of pastoral care as shepherding is well known. What is not often explicitly noted in this connection is the fact that the psalms, especially Psalm 23, are the major biblical source of this shepherd image. In *The Christian Shepherd,* Hiltner says that the basic principles of shepherding are two: communicating concern and acceptance, and contributing to clarification and judgment.[24] The first principle involves allowing counselees to express negative feelings. The second involves helping counselees clarify their conflicting feelings and submit this conflict to God's judgment. Good shepherding is especially evident when the counselor allows expression of negative feelings and does not insist that the counselee take a positive view of the situation.

Hiltner does not explore the Bible's role in this twofold process of shepherding, but the counseling case that he chooses to illustrate these two principles involves the pastor's use of Psalm 23. In this case, Hiltner is critical of the pastor's decision to read the whole psalm to the counselee because the basic motive behind this Bible-reading was the pastor's desire to quell the counselee's venting of negative feelings. To use the psalm in this way was to misperceive the counselee's need to express negative feelings, and thus violated the first principle of shepherding. It was also to misunderstand the psalm itself, for Psalm 23 supports the two basic principles of shepherding. It gives vent to negative feelings without fear of reprisal from God ("Even though I walk through the valley of the shadow of death, I fear no evil") and it expresses conflicting feelings without fear of seeming to be contradictory ("Thou preparest a table before me in the presence of my enemies; thou anointest my head with oil").

By suggesting that the psalms reflect the shepherding role, I have begun to address the question: What can we learn from the psalms about pastoral counseling? What do they have to teach the pastoral counselor? Hiltner, Oates, and Wise do not address this question in any systematic way. They recognize the affinity between the psalms and their own views of counseling, but they do not explore it in any depth. Moreover, their comments on the psalms do not reflect much concern for the formal characteristics of the psalm. Take Hiltner's interpretation of Psalm 38. Should the psalmist have been more specific about the nature of the sin committed, as Hiltner suggests, or is this typical of the psalm form? Is the psalmist's "preoccupation with blame" an inability to accept personal responsibility for what has happened, or is this also typical of the psalm form? If these are typical of the psalm as a form, we should not center on the personal strengths and weaknesses of this psalmist, but on the form itself, and *its* strengths and weaknesses.

We need to address questions of this kind to understand adequately the role that psalms can play in shaping the counseling process. What follows, therefore, is an exploration of modern biblical scholarship on the psalm form, with particular emphasis on the psalm of lament. This exploration of the lament will enable us to see how the psalm may shape the grief counseling process—its methods, objectives, and counselor-counselee relationship.

RECENT BIBLICAL SCHOLARSHIP ON THE PERSONAL LAMENT

The Structure of the Lament

Biblical scholars agree that the book of Psalms consists of various types of psalms, each having its own form or structure. No two experts agree on the number of types, or on all the psalms that belong to each type. But there is general agreement that the following types are the most common: psalms of lament, both personal and communal; psalms of penitence; songs of thanksgiving and praise; songs of trust; and wisdom psalms. All scholars agree that psalms of lament far outnumber any other type, and that individual or personal laments are more numerous than communal laments. Bernhard W. Anderson lists 42 psalms that are personal laments, 2 psalms in which large portions are personal laments, and 7 psalms that are personal laments but are usually classified as psalms of penitence.[25] Moreover, Hermann Gunkel views songs of trust as a subtype of individual laments. If we accept this view, this would mean that well over one third of the psalms can be considered personal laments. Also, while there are many other laments in the Hebrew Bible, the largest number of personal laments is in the book of Psalms.

Claus Westermann suggests that there were three stages in the historical development of the lament. First, there were the short laments that are preserved only in narrative accounts (such as Gen. 25:22 and 27:46; and Judges 15:18 and 21:2). Next came the rhythmically structured laments of the Psalms, the book of Lamentations, and the prophetic books (such as the laments of the nation in Jeremiah 14–15 and Isaiah 63–64, and the laments of the individual in Jeremiah 11–20). Finally, there were the prose prayers in Ezra 9 and Nehemiah 9. The laments in the book of Psalms "can be distinguished from the earlier, very short laments (as encountered in the patriarchal narratives and in the historical accounts) and from the later prose prayers by their characteristic form—a form which evolved out of the worship tradition of psalms of lament."[26]

The Formal Structure of the Lament

The psalms of lament have a characteristic form that allows an unlimited number of variations but requires a fixed sequence of elements. Anderson identifies six elements in this form:

1. *Address to God.* The lament begins with an address to God. This is usually a brief cry for help, but is occasionally expanded into a statement of praise or recollection of God's help in the past.

2. *Complaint.* The lament continues with an expression of one's complaint or problem. In personal laments, the problem is typically sickness, threat of enemies, or fear of death. The complaint is often accompanied by a protestation of personal innocence, that one has done nothing to deserve the suffering one is having to endure. However, in penitential psalms, a subgroup of personal laments, the complaint is one's awareness of personal sin.

3. *Confession of Trust.* Following the complaint, there is

an expression of confidence in God in spite of one's current difficulties. This is often introduced with the word "but" or "nevertheless" and reflects a turning point in the psalmist's view of the situation.

4. *Petition.* Having expressed confidence in God, the psalmist next makes specific appeals to God for intervention and deliverance from present difficulty. Sometimes the petition cites reasons why God should help—for example, the petitioner's innocence, the petitioner's confession of guilt, God's faithfulness in the past, God's commitment to the petitioner and not the petitioner's adversaries, and so forth.

5. *Words of Assurance.* The psalmist next expresses certainty that this petition will be heard. Since such expressions usually mark a rather abrupt shift in the psalm, biblical scholars have given much attention to it. Some suggest that, in the Temple worship, the priest responded to the petition and that the words of assurance reflect this priestly response. While it is impossible to know what this priestly response may have been, it is assumed that it was an assurance that God had heard the petitioner's request.

6. *Vow to Praise.* The lament concludes with the psalmist's vow to testify to the name of God for what has been done in the supplicant's behalf.

Psalm 71 illustrates the six elements of the lament form. It begins with the *address to God* in which the psalmist asks for help:

> ¹ In thee, O LORD, do I take refuge; let me never be put to shame! ² In thy righteousness deliver me and rescue me; incline thy ear to me, and save me! ³ Be thou to me a rock of refuge, a strong fortress, to save me, for thou art my rock and my fortress.

The psalm continues with the *complaint* in which the psalmist, in a very brief statement, describes his problem:

> ⁴ Rescue me, O my God, from the hand of the wicked, from the grasp of the unjust and cruel man.

Next, there follows a *confession of trust* which, in this case, includes a review of God's help in the past:

> ⁵ For thou, O Lord, art my hope, my trust, O LORD, from my youth. ⁶ Upon thee I have leaned from my birth; thou art he who took me from my mother's womb. My praise is continually of thee. ⁷ I have been as a portent to many; but thou art my strong refuge. ⁸ My mouth is filled with thy praise, and with thy glory all the day.

After this confession of trust in God, the psalmist moves into the *petition.* Here he makes a direct appeal for God's help in dealing with those who treat him unjustly and cruelly:

> ⁹ Do not cast me off in the time of old age; forsake me not when my strength is spent. ¹⁰ For my enemies speak concerning me, those who watch for my life consult together, ¹¹ and say, "God has forsaken him; pursue and seize him, for there is none to deliver him." ¹² O God, be not far from me; O my God, make haste to help me! ¹³ May my accusers be put to shame and consumed; with scorn and disgrace may they be covered who seek my hurt.

After this petition, the psalmist utters very brief *words of assurance*—"But I will hope continually"—and then moves immediately into the final segment of the psalm, the *vow to praise.* Since the assurance segment is very short, this brief hiatus between the petition and the vow to praise supports the view that there was a priestly response to the petition that is not actually verbalized in the psalm itself:

> ¹⁴ But I will hope continually, and will praise thee yet more and more. ¹⁵ My mouth will tell of thy righteous acts, of thy deeds of salvation all the day, for their number is past my knowledge. ¹⁶ With the mighty deeds of the Lord GOD I will come, I will praise thy righteousness, thine alone.

The psalm continues in this vow to praise to the end, concluding with the promise:

[24] And my tongue will talk of thy righteous help all the day long, for they have been put to shame and disgraced who sought to do me hurt.

Certain elements of this lament structure have evoked much critical discussion among biblical scholars. Westermann takes particular note of the abrupt shift from petition to assurance, suggesting that in this "reversal from lament to trust and praise of God we are dealing with . . . an activity of God which actually had been experienced and which was concretized, as a result of such experience, in the structure of these psalms." If this sudden reversal is due to some direct experience of God, it is unclear what this experience was. As indicated, some scholars believe that words of assurance were spoken by a priest at this point in the singing of the psalm in the Temple worship. But other scholars believe that an individual, on reaching the safety of the Temple, has already experienced God's protection from enemy pursuit or harassment.

Whatever the historical context of this sudden reversal, there is general agreement among scholars that, as Westermann puts it, "the psalms themselves . . . present only the one side of what was happening—the prayer of those who lamented. The answers given by servants of God (priests or sanctuary prophets) are not in themselves reproduced in most of these psalms. They do, however, indicate changes, reversals, breaks in the laments—which are understandable only when one realizes that the supplicants received answers from outside themselves." But Westermann also warns that these sudden shifts and reversals ought not to be exaggerated. He stresses the "psychological unity" of the whole process of lamentation, noting that petition is already implicit in lamentation, and assurance is already implicit in petition. Thus, the abrupt shift from petition to assurance reflects the fact that transition is built into the very structure of the lament: "This transition in the structure of the psalm of lament is rooted in the lament's function as an appeal. Because the lament is directed toward the one who can change suffering, the change occurs in the psalm or at least it is implied. . . . Understood in this way, the structure of the psalm of lament, which enables us to see the path leading to an alleviation of suffering, is one of the most powerful witnesses to the experience of God's activity in the Old Testament."

Another major concern of biblical scholars is the psalmist's failure to reveal the circumstances behind the complaint. If the historical situation behind *communal* laments is impossible to ascertain, it is equally fruitless to search for the personal circumstances that give rise to the *individual* lament, because the psalmist fails to identify these circumstances. In his analysis of Psalm 13, Westermann points out that the psalms simply are not designed to provide this information: "We never learn what was disturbing the suppliant. The threefold lament does not even give a clue. We never even learn this information in psalms of lament which are much more detailed than Psalm 13. Only in a very few are the symptoms of the suffering described more clearly." Moreover, while we can infer that some psalms of lament concern physical illness, we cannot rule out the possibility that the cry, "Heal me," is being used metaphorically. The plea that God will "vindicate me" or "plead my cause" does not necessarily mean that one has been accused or sentenced. In laments over sin, the nature of the sin is never really identified.

This tendency to express one's complaint in nonspecific terms sheds light on Psalm 38. As we saw, Pastor Weems criticized the psalmist for his failure to be specific about the nature of his sin. In noting this fact, Weems inadvertently recognized a central feature of the lament. The form itself discourages specific personal references. In Anderson's view, "the main question to ask about any psalm is not the situation in the life of David or in the life of some unknown individual which occasioned the composition. . . . Rather, the important question is the purpose of the psalm, and usually this question leads to an inquiry into the psalm's *situation in worship.*" The psalm fails to reveal the circumstances behind the complaint, but this makes it applicable to the experience of many worshipers. Thus, Arkwright's "companionship of feelings" with the psalmist is a use of the psalm that was anticipated by the people of Israel, and made possible by virtue of its general applicability. The psalmist's failure to be specific about the nature of the sin might appear to be a personal weakness, but this is a formal characteristic of the lament that enables other persons to identify with the original lamenter.

Throughout history, this formal characteristic of the lament has enabled millions of readers to apply the psalms to their particular situations. An example is William Bridges' *A Lifting Up for the Downcast,* a set of thirteen sermons preached in 1648 on Psalm 42:11: "Why are you cast down, O my soul, and why are you disquieted within me? Hope in God; for I shall again praise him, my help and my God." In these sermons, Bridges identifies the various conditions that might give rise to this disquiet, including great sins, weak grace, miscarriage of duties, lack of assurance, temptation, desertion, affliction, inability to work, and discouragements due to the condition itself.[27] Some of these conditions might have appeared on the psalmist's own list of complaints, but those relating to typical Puritan interests would not. This underscores the fact that the psalms can speak to conditions that were not anticipated by the psalmist, nor, for that matter, by seventeenth-century Puritans. The counselee's question of the counselor, "Is this what the psalmist means, or am I reading my feelings into it?" can be answered as follows: "You may be reading your own feelings into it, but this is precisely what the psalm invites and encourages."

A more troublesome feature of the psalm of lament for biblical scholars is the fact that many psalms pray for vindication against one's enemies. Some psalms (including Psalms 35; 59; 69; 70; 109; 137; 140) are called "cursing psalms" because they cry for vengeance against one's enemies. To Christians who take seriously Jesus' injunction to "pray for those who persecute you," this feature of the lament is particularly disturbing. Hiltner touched on this problem in his assessment of the Arkwright case when he commended Pastor Weems for soft-pedaling the psalmist's "paranoid" feelings, his "intense and circular preoccupation with blame." Since the cry for vindication is a typical feature of the psalm of lament and is not a psychological aberration of this particular psalmist, criticism of this aspect of the psalm must be directed at the form itself.

How should we view this feature of the lament? Anderson says that we need to keep three things in mind. First, while the psalm contains traces of ancient curse formulas, they are not curses in the proper sense; the psalmist does not expect that his words will have a direct or immediate effect on his victim. Rather, "they are really prayers to God who obtains vindication in his own way and in his own time." Second, the psalms wrestle with the problems of human existence within the context of this life (the "threescore and ten" of Ps. 90:10) and they concentrate on the problems of life *now* with a fierce and passionate intensity: "The psalmists do not take seriously the possibility that the imbalances of life will somehow be corrected in another form of existence beyond our historical experience." Thus, the psalmist curses his enemies now because he cannot expect that they will eventually be punished in the hereafter. Third, the cry for vengeance is predicated on the fact that God and the people of Israel have entered into a covenant relationship, so that *their* enemies are *God*'s enemies, and God is therefore expected to do something about these enemies. The covenant relationship demands it.

We cannot excise the cry for vengeance from the psalms. But these three considerations help us to understand the beliefs and convictions that legitimated it. When viewed from the pastoral counseling perspective, this cry for vengeance can be understood as the venting of negative feelings, and thus an initial step in the process of positive change. Counselees today would undoubtedly make greater use of the cry for vengeance if there were not such strong social sanctions against it, and if they had confidence that the pastor could genuinely accept these negative feelings. The pastoral counseling movement has often cited *anger* as an example of negative feelings that require venting. The cry for vengeance is an even stronger negative feeling, and reflects the fact that the *range* and *depth* of negative feelings acceptable in the lament is broader and more intense than is often encouraged in pastoral counseling. Pastors often allow only a certain respectable range and depth of expression of negative feelings. When the counselee goes beyond these limits, the pastor feels a corresponding decrease in empathy toward the counselee and increase in irritation and suspicion. Counselees' cries for vengeance against their enemies elicit the response, "Perhaps you are overreacting a bit," or "It's not easy to be forgiving." The pastor in such cases is basically sympathetic but has not "really accepted" the counselee's feelings. Unless a pastor can say, "Considering what he did to you, he should have to suffer for a long time to come" or "I can't see how you could forgive him for what he's done to you," the pastor will fall short of the empathy that the psalmists expected when they addressed their laments to God.

A related problem is the fact that, in some laments, the psalmist claims personal innocence. Westermann notes that Christians have difficulty with this because they are heavily influenced by Paul's view that "sinfulness is a part of man's condition and that the confession of sin is therefore a part of every approach to God. From the standpoint of the Pauline doctrine there can be no lament without a confession of sin; if a lamenter appears before God, he appears as one who is guilty." Westermann points out, however, that the psalmist can claim innocence because the issue is a specific offense, not the psalmist's general condition. Thus, the modern-day Christian feels that there is something unseemly in protesting one's innocence before God, but the psalmists consider it quite appropriate to remind God of their innocence and to assert: "I have done no wrong in this case, yet I am being made to suffer. Why?"

Perhaps here as well, pastoral counselors need to give more attention to this aspect of the lament. Many counselees have not felt free to express feelings of self-justification because they have been taught that their condition is one of sinfulness before God. The psalm of lament may be general and unspecific about the *circumstances* behind the complaint, but its protest of innocence is quite specific. It relates to a specific act or event, not to the general innocence of the lamenter. This distinction can be most useful in counseling. Christian pastors believe that all persons are sinful and in need of God's forgiving grace. But this does not mean that the pastor cannot "accept" a counselee's protest of innocence in a specific situation. Instead of the suspicious, "Maybe there was something you did, sort of unintentionally, that contributed to this," the pastor ought to be able to say with conviction, "There's no question you had nothing to do with this. It's not your fault."

The Lament of the Mediator

Now that we have the basic structure of the personal lament before us, I want to consider an important variation. This is the lament of the mediator, a variation on the personal lament having extremely important implications for pastoral counseling. Westermann points out that, while the lamenter is usually the one who is personally suffering pain and loss, there are times when the lamenter is someone else. This normally occurs when a personal lament deals with matters facing the nation: "The individual brings before God not his own personal suffering but, through his mediation, the suffering which affects the nation." Historically, this lament of the mediator "first appears in the lament of Moses, recurs in the lament of Elisha and reaches a high point in the laments (or confessions) of Jeremiah, which then in turn point to the songs of the Suffering Servant in Deutero-Isaiah. Thus, the history of God's relationship with Israel begins with the lament of the oppressed in Egypt and reaches its climax in the suffering of one who mediates in behalf of the nation."

Westermann notes that the lament of the mediator has many of the same characteristics of the personal lament. Thus, Jeremiah's lament for the nation employs three of the major elements of the personal lament: the *address to God,* which includes an accusation against God; the *complaint* (Westermann calls it the *I-lament*), which expresses the loneliness and inescapability of his situation; and the *petition,* which pleads for God's intervention against the enemies of his prophetic mission. In this lament, Jeremiah's concern is not for himself but for his prophetic mission. His accusation against God is a reproach of God "for the unbearable tension which he had to endure between his mission on the one hand and the absence of any realization of his message on the other." The I-lament expresses his complaint that his preaching has brought him only loneliness, disgrace, and contempt. His petition to God asks for help against enemies who want to "lay a trap" for him in order to silence his announcement of judgment.

This lament of the mediator relates to pastoral counseling

in two important ways. First of all, it makes clear that counseling which deals with human suffering is never far removed from prophetic ministry. While "pastoral" and "prophetic" ministry are sometimes seen as two distinct types of ministry, it is important that the psalmist's personal lament anticipates the prophet's mediatorial lament, and that these laments have the same core elements of address to God: complaint and petition. Thus, to the extent that pastoral counseling is shaped by the personal lament, it is the crucible in which prophetic ministry takes form.[28]

In the second place, the lament of the mediator indicates that counselors who deal with human suffering cannot help raising their own laments to God in the sufferer's behalf. They are not the ones who are immediately suffering, but they agonize with the counselee and lament in the counselee's behalf. The counselee's accusation against God becomes the counselor's accusation against God. The counselee's frustration and discouragement become the counselor's frustration and discouragement. The counselee's enemy, whether a personal enemy like a contentious family member or a devious work associate, or an impersonal enemy like alcohol or incurable illness, becomes the counselor's enemy.

The lament of the mediator suggests, in other words, that the pastoral counselor is a "suffering servant." In the 1950s and early 1960s, many pastors viewed their counseling role as that of the "suffering servant" who does not react to the counselee's conflicted feelings as a detached observer, but enters into them in a deeply empathic way. Since this view of the pastoral counselor is now in something of an eclipse,[29] perhaps it can be revitalized by according to the lament of the mediator a significant role in pastoral counseling.

However, if the lament of the mediator is to serve as a basis for the recovery of this emphasis in pastoral counseling, we need to take into consideration certain changes in this type of lament that are reflected in the Suffering Servant songs of Deutero-Isaiah. Westermann says: "Between the suffering and death of Jesus and the suffering in the laments of Jeremiah stand the songs of the Suffering Servant in Deutero-Isaiah." These songs reflect a "revolution in the lament of the mediator which occurs between the laments of Jeremiah and the Servant Songs," a revolution attributable to the intervening collapse of the state, the temple, and the empire. This revolution reflects major changes in the lament of the mediator. In the first place, the "I-lament" becomes not just agonizing over the sufferings of others, or even personal identification with these sufferings, but "substitutionary suffering" where "the suffering of a single man takes on far-reaching and positive significance for the wellbeing of a whole people." In the second place, "accusation against the enemy recedes into the background; the transgressor is included in the supplication of the mediator (Isa. 53:12)."

These two changes in the lament of the mediator have direct implications for the recovery of the suffering servant emphasis in pastoral counseling. The first of these changes means that the pastor's role is not only to participate in the sufferings of grieving individuals. For the pastor's mediatorial role also involves confronting death, through regular involvement in funerals and related pastoral acts, in behalf of the whole people of God.

The second of these changes means that pastoral counseling cannot be content with enabling the counselee to express vindictive feelings toward personal and impersonal enemies, essential as this venting of negative feelings is. The counselor also needs to help the counselee realize that God is prepared to forgive these enemies. God's willingness to forgive is not an expression of disloyalty to the counselee. It is an initial step in the healing process, and thus also commended to the counselee when he is prepared to take this step.

The Lament of God

A second major variation on the personal lament also has great significance for pastoral counseling. This concerns the lament of God, a revolutionary development in the lament found in the prophetic books of Isaiah, Hosea, and Jeremiah. Westermann points out that these books include songs in which God laments over the people's rebellion and the judgment that must be brought against them. These laments testify to the fact that God is "wrestling" with himself. God mourns the suffering and destruction of his people, even as he gives them over into the hands of their enemies. Thus, "the juxtaposition of God's wrath and God's grief vis-à-vis his people in these texts is almost incomprehensible. This isn't something that is said all the time, but only when life is pushed to its ultimate limit: to the edge of annihilation which God brings upon his own people. The lament of God is not a general statement about God; it is rather only one of those rare and extreme possibilities for speaking of God. As such, it finds its ground in the situation itself. The incomprehensible idea that God destroys his own has its corollary in that which is equally incomprehensible, viz., that the God of wrath is also the God who mourns." Westermann concludes that, with the laments of God found in Jeremiah, the "doctrine of the incarnation could take on new meaning." The God who assumes human form would be understood in terms of the history of his relationship with his people, a history "which ultimately reaches the point where God, as the God of judgment, suffers for his people."

The lament of God has major implications for pastoral counseling. As Westermann observes, "It is certainly not by chance that [the laments of God] stand beside Jeremiah's own laments." This picture of God lamenting alongside the human sufferer is central to grief counseling. The counselee's lament gains its meaning, ultimately, from the fact that God shares this lament.

THE LAMENT AND GRIEF COUNSELING

The Structure of the Grief Experience

How might the personal lament and its two major variations shape the grief counseling process—its methods, its objectives, its counselor-counselee relationship? As we take up this question, it is important to note that the two variations on the lament do not involve fundamental changes in its form or structure. The variations that they introduce are not in the form of the lament (its six sequential elements) but in the identity of the speaker of the lament. The lament was originally spoken by the immediate sufferer, but these later variations introduced new lamenters—first the mediator and then God himself. Since the basic form of the lament remains intact throughout these developments, I will focus attention on the form and explore its implications for pastoral counseling. Specifically, I want to show how the lament can shape the counseling process by forming our experience of grief. This discussion will center on a major article on the psalm of lament by Walter Brueggemann, entitled "The Formfulness of Grief."[30]

Brueggemann points out that ancient Israel "devised typical patterns of speech and expression to articulate various needs, hopes and experiences of the community. While the experience certainly shaped the pattern of expression, it is also true that the pattern of expression helped to shape the experience, so that it could be received, understood, and coped with." Among these experience-shaping patterns of speech, the "form of lament is clearly one of the dominant forms of community expression in the life of Israel. Certain characteristic ways of speech had an intimate relationship to situations of misery, hurt, and agony. And an understanding of the form will help us understand both how Israel's faith understood and experienced hurt and how it interpreted it in the context of her faith."

Brueggemann contends that the basic *intention* of the lament is to rehabilitate and restore those who are suffering, and the *form* of the lament helps to realize this objective. It does this when it *"enhances* experience and brings it to articulation and also *limits* the experience of suffering so that it can be received and coped with according to the perspectives, perceptions, and resources of the community." Thus, the form of the lament defines the experience of suffering: "It tells the experiencer the shape of the experience which it is legitimate to experience." What makes the lament effective in dealing with situations of misery, hurt and agony is the fact that it provides a *form* for understanding and experiencing these miseries, hurts, and agonies: "The form not only describes what is, but articulates what is expected and insisted upon."

In Brueggemann's view, we moderns find it difficult to appreciate this formative influence of the psalm of lament because we lack the forms that enable us to understand our experiences of grief: "Technical medicine, like urban consciousness generally, is resistant to form, denies the formfulness of experiences, and resists the notion that grief or any other experience is formful." Elisabeth Kübler-Ross's view that the death-grief process includes five elements *(denial and isolation, anger, bargaining, depression,* and *acceptance)* is an attempt to recover the formfulness of the grief experience.[31] But while Brueggemann supports her effort to describe the formfulness of this experience, and recognizes similarities between the lament and her stages (the major parallel is that both allow expression of anger), he emphasizes the very significant differences between them. (See the chart on page 75 for purposes of comparison.) The differences are due primarily to the fact that the lament expresses confidence in God's ability to intervene in the life of his people. Thus, the major dissimilarity in the two structures is that *confession of trust* leads to *petition* at precisely the point where, in Kübler-Ross's structure, *bargaining* is followed by *depression.* This

STAGES IN THE GRIEF PROCESS

Psalm of Lament	Kübler-Ross
Address to God	Denial and Isolation
Complaint	Anger
Confession of Trust	Bargaining
Petition	Depression
Words of Assurance	Acceptance
Vow to Praise	

major structural difference has a very decisive effect on the subsequent elements in the sequence. The lament moves from petition to confidence and praise, while Kübler-Ross's model moves from depression to acceptance.

Brueggemann acknowledges that this move from depression to acceptance marks a shift as dramatic as when the lament moves from petition to confidence. But "it is unclear concerning Kübler-Ross whether 'acceptance' is affirmation or whether it is resignation. I believe she, herself, is not clear." In the case of the lament, "the form itself centers in intervention, whereas Kübler-Ross must treat the intervention ambiguously and gingerly because the context of modernity must by definition screen it out." When the grieving or dying person is able to move from depression to acceptance, this is usually because of the support of a friend, relative or member of the medical health team. Such intervention, no matter how consoling, lacks "the presence of a sovereign God" who can "powerfully intrude to transform."

Brueggemann's purpose is not to criticize those who are engaged in charting the stages of grief and dying.[32] Rather, his intention is to illustrate how, for ancient Israel, it was the *form* of the lament that made possible the "transforming intervention" of God. Contemporary stage theories of grief and dying differ most from the lament in their failure to include this transformative dimension in the grief experience itself. Why they do not do so is less a reflection on the personal convictions of these authors and more a commentary on the fact that modern consciousness and its ideologies (including psychological ideologies) resist the *limitations* that traditional forms such as the lament place on human experience. For moderns, the form of the lament is simply too structured, its movement from complaint to petition to assurance to praise is too predictably pat. The very ambiguity that Brueggemann sees in Kübler-Ross's stage of *acceptance* is reflective of the desire of moderns for forms that are open-ended, their outcome clothed in mystery.

But while the basic structure of the traditional lament did not change, this is not to say that the lament was a rigid form. In the course of time, its cry for vengeance against one's enemies was accompanied by petition in their behalf. Also, the personal lament was augmented by the lament of the mediator and the lament of God. The lament of God was an especially significant development, because it simultaneously *enhanced* the lamenter's experience of God and severely *limited* the lament's effectiveness in making the grief experience comprehensible. In my judgment, the lament of God enables the traditional lament form to articulate with the ambiguity of modern consciousness while retaining the traditional model's capacity to "powerfully intrude to transform" the experience of loss. Thus, while Brueggemann's warning against our easy acceptance of "the frames of reference of the psychological disciplines which are insensitive to form" is thoroughly appropriate, we should avoid the opposite error of assuming that the alternative choice is a rigid traditional form. In point of fact, the traditional lament form was not invulnerable to changing conditions in human experience. One reason that the personal lament form has survived for so many centuries is that the original form was not specific about the conditions that gave rise to the psalmist's lament, enabling it to adapt itself to new circumstances that were unanticipated by the early psalmists. Another, and more profound, reason for its survival was that it was augmented by new variations (the lament of the mediator and the lament of God), changes that introduced new complexities and ambiguities into its original form.

What are the implications of Brueggemann's comparison of the traditional lament with Kübler-Ross's stages for pastoral counseling? In my view, this comparison of the "formfulness" of the lament with the relative "formlessness" of Kübler-Ross's stages points to the fact that pastors have given inadequate attention to helping the grieving give "form" to this experience. If grief counseling is to be shaped by the psalm of lament, it needs to deepen its understanding of the *complaint* stage and take seriously the three later stages in the lament: *petition, words of assurance,* and *vow to praise.* These later stages are especially important because, as Brueggemann shows, they reflect the "transforming intervention" of God. But this intervention gains its entry through the *complaint* stage, so the importance of this stage can hardly be exaggerated. Thus, I want to comment on each of these four stages, relating them to corresponding phases and objectives in the counseling process.

The Complaint in Grief Counseling

The first lesson we can learn from taking the lament form seriously is the importance of sensitizing ourselves to the *range* and *depth* of complaints in the grief experience. When applied to grief, Kübler-Ross's stage theory would have us be attentive to the grieving person's *anger,* and much pastoral counseling literature has focused on the grieving person's *guilt.* These are two of the most important "negative" feelings that lie behind the complaints of the grieving. Feelings of another type that lie behind these complaints are "positive" feelings of self-justification, defending the integrity of one's attitudes and behavior toward the deceased during his or her lifetime. Often, these two types of feelings are expressed simultaneously, and the grieving person seems to be reacting to the death in contradictory ways. This apparent contradiction underscores the fact that the grieving person has a whole range of feelings about the death he or she has recently experienced, and that they are very difficult to sort out.

Complaints arise out of this welter of feelings, and are the grieving person's attempt to focus these feelings, to give them a "name." What kinds of complaints typically emerge out of these negative and self-justifying feelings? Some complaints relate to the circumstances of the death, and are concerned with whether it was untimely and/or could have been averted. Psalms of lament focus on these circumstantial matters when they chide God for failing to act against one's enemies and suggest that he could have done something about it. But the deeper and more intense complaints of the grieving are not circumstantial, but relational. They concern the effect of the death on the relationship between the survivors and the person who has died, and between the individual survivors. Many psalms of lament also focus on these relational complaints, and typically center on the question: "Whom may I trust in this time of suffering and loss?" "Are you my friend, or are you my enemy?" In the grief experience, this question is asked of the persons with whom one associates, of the deceased, of God, and even of oneself, for it is quite possible for us to betray our own trust.

In grief, many relational complaints center on this question of trust. When addressed to other people with whom one associates, these complaints are typical: "He made no effort to understand what I was going through." "She tried to cover up the loss with superficial pleasantries." "All they care about is the money he left them." "They'll never appreciate what I went through during her illness." When addressed to the deceased, the following complaints are not uncommon: "You are now free, and I am left with the task of carrying on." "You left our affairs in such a mess, I'll never get them straightened out." "Why do you go on condemning me?" "Why do you seem so close and yet so elusively far away?" When addressed to God, the following complaints are often raised: "Why did you take her now?" "Where were you when I most needed you?" "Why was he put through such terrible agony?" "Did you cause her death, or merely acquiesce in it?" "It seems so utterly senseless." When addressed to oneself, these are typical complaints: "I expected to be sad and depressed, but not irritable like this." "Why does my faith desert me at times like this?" "I'm taking this badly; I feel like my own worst enemy." "Why do I have trouble grieving; am I made of stone?" "Why am I trying so desperately to hold on to her?" "I let him down when he was dying and needed understanding."

The grieving person who finds adequate grounds for trust, whether from other persons, the deceased, God, or self, will be able to move to the next stage of the grief process, the *confession of trust.* Those who do not, need to be helped to discover such grounds for trust. The pastoral conversation can itself provide a context in which trust is not only discussed but actually experienced. If grounds for trust are not established in time, the effect is likely to be a deep, pervasive bitterness or the more subtle but no less damaging sense of disillusionment. The presence or absence of trust should not, however, be understood in grandiose terms. It is not the answer to one's complaints or the end to one's suffering, but a simple confidence that one will be able to cope.

The Petition in Grief Counseling

The second lesson we can learn from taking the form of the lament seriously is the importance of *petitioning* God to intervene. The bereaved often voice this petition, typically in a hesitant though hopeful way, but pastors sometimes fail to hear it. One reason for this is that they want the counselee to move toward the *acceptance* of the loss, while the counselee's desire to petition is *prima facie* evidence that he or she is not yet disposed to accept the loss. Another reason they neglect it is that Kübler-Ross places so much emphasis on *bargaining,* which occurs in her theory in place of the confession of trust, the stage that immediately precedes the petition in the traditional lament. Her use of the term "bargaining" tends to reduce petition to acts of desperation or manipulation (the opposite of trust), and pastors influenced by Kübler-Ross tend as a result to discount the counselee's petitions as futile attempts to "bargain" with God. But many typical petitions by the bereaved are not attempts to bargain with God. They are thoroughly legitimate requests for God's help: "Remove my anger, loneliness, frustration, sense of betrayal." "Help me understand the meaning of my loss. It seems entirely meaningless to me now." "Remove my guilt for things I ought not to have said and done, and for things I ought to have said and done but did not." "Help me cope with an uncertain future." "Give me courage in this dark hour." While the bereaved do not always express these concerns in clear petitionary form, these petitions are frequently present. Petition has great importance for the grief process. It enables one to do something about one's complaints by clarifying how they might be alleviated, and by laying hold of new spiritual energies to overcome them.

Consider the case of the sixty-eight-year-old woman who had recently lost her husband. When her pastor came to visit her, she wanted to talk about the responsibilities of taking care of the house, and described in considerable detail how she had had to call a carpenter in the middle of the night to repair a leaking water heater. At no point in this conversation did she petition God to relieve her of these heavy responsibilities or ask him to help her cope with them. But when the pastor prayed at the conclusion of the visit, asking God to stretch out his "guiding hand to steady our walk in life," she confessed, "I am anxious about tomorrow," and then after crying briefly, she said, "There is the steadying hand. I'll be all right." There was an unspoken petition in this woman's voice throughout the conversation ("Help me cope with the new responsibilities that my husband's death has thrust upon me") and, at the end of the visit, she expressed some confidence, albeit tentative, that God would provide the assistance she needed in the days and weeks ahead.[33]

The petitions of the dying person are also more than mere bargainings. The dying person who says, "If God would make it possible for me to walk out of this hospital tomorrow, I would attend church every Sunday the rest of my life," knows that regular church attendance is hardly adequate payment for this new lease on life. If this is a bargain, God certainly gets the short end of it! But consider the man whom Peter healed at the Beautiful Gate (Acts 3:1–10). This man did not go with Peter and John into the Temple, "walking and praising God," because he felt this would settle a bargain he had made with God during his years of infirmity. Why, then, must we say that the vow to attend church each Sunday if one's health is restored is "bargaining" with God? When we say this, we hear the second half of the patient's statement ("I will attend church every Sunday") and call this vow "bargaining," but hearing the first half would enable us to recognize that what we have here is petition, "If God would make it possible . . ." Thus, even this seemingly crass instance of what Kübler-Ross would call "bargaining" is a petition for God's intervention. Perhaps it is our zeal to help the dying move toward "acceptance" that causes us to dismiss these petitions as mere bargainings. Or is it that we moderns have difficulty believing that a promise to attend church if one is healed might be the petitioner's way of *vowing to praise?* The author of Acts does not question the fact that the beggar's joyful entry into the Temple after being healed was for the purpose of praising God.

The Words of Assurance in Grief Counseling

A third counseling lesson we can learn from taking the *form* of the lament seriously concerns the *words of assurance* that follow the *petition.* As we have seen, many biblical scholars believe that assurance of God's help was actually communicated by the priest or sanctuary prophet. We *might* conclude from this that the counselor's role is also a priestly one, that is, to assure the counselee that his or her petition has been heard and is even now being acted on by God. I would not want to discount the potential value of such assurance from the counselor. There is the danger, however, that it will be misunderstood or rejected by the counselee. As Westermann points out, even though the words of assurance were spoken by a human voice, what was critical to the movement from petition to assurance that one's petition had been heard was not human words but the *experience* of God's trustworthiness, which is implicit in the very structure of the lament itself. Thus, "because the lament is directed toward the one who can change suffering, the change occurs in the psalm or at least it is implied. . . . Understood in this way, the structure of the psalm of lament, which enables us to see the path leading to an alleviation of suffering, is one of the most powerful witnesses to the experience of God's activity."

Verbal assurance from the pastor that the counselee's petition has been heard cannot take the place of the *experience* of God's intervention. However, if we shift our attention from the Temple priest to the lament of the mediator, the counselor may serve as a *mediator* in support of the counselee's petition. This means making the counselee's petition one's own. As with the I-lament of Jeremiah, the pastor needs to sustain not only the counselee's complaint but also the counselee's petition to God.

There are times, of course, when the pastor has difficulty making the counselee's petition his or her own. The pastor who says, "I too pray that God will return your husband to you," is contributing to a denial of the reality of the death. But this pastor can certainly share the underlying intent of this petition, making the agony and longing that prompt it his or her own—"If only you could have him back . . ." The pastor can also help the counselee clarify in what sense she may indeed "have him back" and begin to experience this "return." David Switzer points out, for example, that one of the needs of the bereaved is "the resurrection of the deceased within the self." He suggests that the conversation between the pastor and the bereaved can contribute to this "resurrection" because "the language that has been the communicating link with the other, in being heard by the speaker himself as he talks of the person and the relationship, carries with it the emotional power of the relationship and reinforces the internalized living presence of the other."[34] Thus, by being aware of the role that the pastoral conversation itself may play in effecting this internalization of the living presence of the deceased, the pastor is able to identify with even this most "impossible" petition—the return of the dead. In sharing this petition, identifying with the longing and the agony behind it, the counselor helps the counselee experience the "presence" of her husband in a new way. The result is neither mere "acceptance" of her loss nor a denial of the reality of death, but the emergence of a new dimension in the relationship between the deceased and the survivor.

Consider the case of Harry, whose wife had died about ten weeks earlier after suffering from cancer for several years. On the pastor's second pastoral visit after the funeral, Harry said: "She isn't here with me, but yet I can feel her presence all around me. I can do anything but touch her—she seems that close. Do you suppose that's the way God brings us comfort? I keep thinking of her as she was healthy and think less of her in the casket."

Harry recognizes that this new dimension in their relationship was not inevitable. It required divine intervention—the experience of God's activity. But he also recognizes that this answer to his need for comfort was due, in part, to his pastor's active *mediation.* He says that he felt bitter at the funeral when the pastor read the words from the Bible about Jesus sending a comforter, and remembered thinking to himself that nothing could ever comfort him. But now, ten weeks later, he does feel comforted. It was not that he cured himself of grief, or that the pastor cured his grief at the funeral, it was God who did the curing. But having said this, he asks the pastor: "Reverend, would it be all right if I prayed and thanked God for his comfort while you're here? *It's easier to think of him when you're around"* (emphasis added). Harry's grief process has moved from *petition* (for comforting) to *assurance* in part because the pastor supported the petition (shared Harry's prayer for comforting) and helped to mediate Harry's request and God's response. Harry's comment, "It's easier to think of him when you're around," is an indirect acknowledgment of his pastor's mediating role.[35] In a real sense, therefore, the counselor-counselee relationship is based on their sharing of the counselee's petition. It is this sharing that enables the counselor to play a mediating role.

The pastor's suggestion that Christ would send his Comforter draws attention to another possible source of the *assur-*

ance stage of the counseling process. This is that some bereaved persons experience comfort through their trust in Christ. At the time of the funeral, Harry was too "bitter" to accept any form of divine comfort. In terms of the lament form, he was in the *complaint* stage and not yet ready to be comforted. But he could be more accepting of the comfort which Christ offers the bereaved when his grief reached the *petition* stage. How might the pastor help such counselees accept this supportive role of Christ? This can be done through assurances that Christ shares the counselee's petitions. This is often accomplished through prayer at the close of the session or visit. The pastor assures the counselee that Christ supports the petitions of those who trust in him, whether the petition is for comforting, for understanding the meaning of one's loss, for strength to cope with the future, or for relief from feelings of guilt and remorse.

The Vow to Praise in Grief Counseling

A fourth counseling lesson we can learn from the form of the lament concerns the *vow to praise.* The psalm of lament concludes with the vow to testify for what God has done in the supplicant's behalf. It may seem odd that grief counseling would conclude with *praise* of God. Isn't "acceptance" or "resignation" enough to ask of the bereaved? Doesn't "praise of God" demand too much? There are two valid responses to these questions. In the first place, for some who are bereaved, it seems perfectly natural that the grief process will culminate in praise of God because praise is an integral part of their Christian hope: "Why are you cast down, O my soul, and why are you disquieted within me? Hope in God; for I shall again praise him, my help and my God" (Ps. 42:11). Such hope-filled praise may be aided by circumstances (e.g., the death came at the end of a long, fruitful life, or the deceased was spared pain and suffering) or by the beliefs and attitudes of the bereaved (such as confidence that the deceased awaits the bereaved in heaven, or trust that whatever happens in life is for the best). In such cases, we may have confidence that, if the grief process has been shaped by the elements of the lament in proper sequence, this praise of God is genuine and not false bravado or forced piety.

But, in the second place, some people, in spite of having "worked through" their grief, are unable to give praise to God. Does this situation reflect some unresolved bitterness against God? Perhaps so. But some find it difficult to give praise because they do not understand God's role in their loss as meriting praise, blame, or indifference. These persons are more "disillusioned" than bitter. Did God cause the death, or acquiesce in it? Did God have power to intervene, and choose not to? Some who feel that God somehow caused the death or at least chose not to avert it may remain forever resentful toward God. Others may simply "resign" themselves to what has happened and "accept" it as inevitable. These reactions point to another fundamental objective of pastoral counseling with the bereaved, of recognizing that God also laments. One may experience that the God who is capable of destroying is also able to mourn more deeply even than people who grieve. These counselees may not be able to praise God, but they can know experientially that God mourns with them. God intervenes powerfully in mourning with those who grieve and certainly brings consolation. For some who grieve, simply knowing that God mourns with them may be their first experience of hope-giving comfort. If trust in God is a source of new spiritual energies, experiencing God's sorrow may be the beginning of such trust.

It is important, therefore, that pastoral counseling of the bereaved enable the counselee who sees no reason for praising God to experience God's sorrow. This may be communicated in words by the counselor, perhaps through prayer addressed to the "God who mourns the loss of . . ." But however it occurs, the counselee who has difficulty praising God needs to sense God's own acceptance of this very difficulty. God's acceptance of this resistance is a striking feature of the concluding section of many psalms of lament. God seems to say to the bereaved, "If I were in your shoes, and you in mine, I would have difficulty praising you."

Finally, this divine acceptance of one's reluctance to praise provides a model for another goal in counseling, that of forgiving others. In grief counseling, one important sign that the counselee is using new spiritual energies is that recriminations against those who "caused" the death (incompetent doctors, slow ambulance team, the drunken driver) and charges that the deceased contributed to his or her own death (such as failure to see a doctor, poor eating habits) are being replaced by conversation about positive experiences in the counselee's life with the deceased. One should not minimize the guilt that people must acknowledge for the deaths of other persons. One should, however, draw attention to the importance of "internalizing" the "living presence" of the deceased. In this process, the agents of death also recede into the background. To the extent that God was included in the counselee's list of "enemies" who might have averted the death, experiencing God's own sorrow over the loss will enable the person to recall those earlier times when God's activity in life was truly joyous and to anticipate future times when God will again evoke spontaneous, unmitigated praise.

The Form of Grief Counseling

To conclude this discussion of the lament and its role in grief counseling, I want to summarize the foregoing discussions of the lament in grief counseling by tracing the counseling process, step by step:

1. *Address to God.* This initial step in the counseling process need not be verbalized. It is based on the fact that the conversation is pastoral, and thus founded on an implicit understanding that not only are the counselor and the counselee talking with each other but also the whole conversation is addressed to God.

2. *Complaint.* The verbalization of the lament begins with the counselee's complaint. This involves the venting of negative feelings, especially of *frustration* and *disillusionment,* and may include cries of vengeance and claims of personal innocence. The pastor's role here is to be "really accepting" of the counselee's negative feelings. If the pastor is not accepting of them, the ability to share the petitions that emerge out of these complaints will be seriously impaired.

3. *Confession of Trust.* In the lament, this is the point where the process, to use Hiltner's apt phrase, begins to "turn the corner." It is the "but" or "nevertheless" that follows the catharsis of negative feeling. In the counseling process, this stage is often unverbalized; it is more likely to be expressed through attitude or mood, the sense that "I must go on" or "I need to get hold of myself."

4. *Petition.* In this stage of the process, the counselee is able to express specific needs, desires, and wants, and to identify those things which are essential to mental, physical, and spiritual survival. In verbalizing these petitions, the counselee gives clearer focus to the sense of trust that was beginning to emerge in the preceding stage but was as yet unfocused. Now the counselee is beginning to place trust and confidence in those things which, if realized, will bring this grief experience to a good resolution (whether these "things" means overcoming loneliness, understanding the meaning of the loss for his or her future, having strength to meet the demands of life, and so forth). The pastor's role here is to help the counselee clarify the petitions, to gain a clear sense of what the petitions are.

5. *Words of Assurance.* In this stage of the process, the movement shifts from the counselee's own efforts to cope with grief to the assurance that one does not have to "go it alone," that the grief is being shared by others. This involves two important initiatives on the counselor's part. First, the counselor makes clear to the counselee that he or she shares the counselee's petitions. Through words or attitude, the counselor conveys, "I too want this for you." This assurance helps to give the counselee a sense of being supported in this time of loss. This is not merely commiseration, but an active and committed support that may well include taking actions outside the pastoral conversation itself to help the counselee realize his or her petition. Second, the counselor helps the counselee to know or sense that God hears these petitions. The counselor not only contributes to the counselee's sense of being supported but also provides a sense of relief—the lifting of a burden that results from knowing that one's petitions are not ignored.

6. *Vow to Praise.* In this stage of the process, the counselee is beginning to sense, in clear and concrete ways, that his or her petitions are being received and that new spiritual energies are being made available. These spiritual forces are reflected, for example, in the internalization of the living presence of the deceased. The counselee begins to experience hope, and with this hope comes the desire to praise God for his help during the counselee's "walk through the valley of the shadow of death." In this stage, there are the initial signs that the counselee is now ready to redirect the energies of hurt and despair toward thoughts and activities that reflect a hopeful attitude toward the future. The counselee who remains bitter toward God may be helped to see that God has deep feelings too, and could hardly have remained unmoved by the counselee's sufferings. The spirit of praise is vitally important to the resolution of grief, because it reinforces the

hope that was rekindled in clarifying one's petitions, and checks the drift toward apathy that typically follows the realization of these petitions. The counselor can foster this spirit of praise, not by viewing it as the counselee's Christian obligation ("In all things and in all ways let us give praise to God"), but by assisting in clarifying what, in this whole experience, invites or warrants praise to God. In the psalm of lament, the psalmist's vow to praise is not general, but quite specific.

This process of grief counseling is schematized in the chart on page 91. The stages do not represent a single counseling session or pastoral visit, but reflect the total process of "working through" the experience of grief.

Throughout this discussion, I have wanted to show that the psalm of lament can guide this process, helping it to move from complaint through petition to assurance and praise. This means, in the first place, that the lament can help define the basic objectives of grief counseling. In the complaint phase of the counseling process, the counselee is encouraged to give vent to negative or self-justifying feelings. But the counselor's objectives do not end with the venting of strong feelings. The ultimate objectives of grief counseling are grounded in the assurance that the counselee's suffering and petitions are shared by others.

In the second place, the psalm of lament clarifies the relationship between counselor and counselee in grief counseling. As mediator between the sufferer and God, the counselor accepts the counselee's negative self-justifying feelings, shares and clarifies the counselee's petitions, and helps the counselee to give concrete expression to his or her praise of God. What the counselor keeps in mind throughout this process is that the role of mediator is not to draw attention to his or her own capacities for providing hope or giving comfort, but to open channels for the "transforming intervention" of God.

THE GRIEF COUNSELING PROCESS

STAGE	COUNSELEE	COUNSELOR
Address to God	Implicit understanding that conversation is addressed to God	Implicit understanding that conversation is addressed to God
Complaint	Gives vent to negative and self-justifying feelings	Helps counselee "name" these feelings in the form of complaints
Confession of Trust	Expresses sense of being upheld and able to cope	Helps counselee identify and cultivate grounds for trust
Petition	Expresses specific needs and desires	Helps counselee clarify and focus petitions
Words of Assurance	Experiences support for petitions and relief from sufferings	Supports counselee's petitions and assures counselee that God hears the prayers of those who lament
Vow to Praise	Experiences response to petitions and begins to hope	Helps counselee clarify grounds for praise; affirms "God who mourns" when counselee cannot praise

In the third place, the psalm of lament reflects the sense in which grief counseling involves a nondirective method. Like many psalms, the grief counseling process is not rigid or forced. Because it has emotional components similar to those of laments, it facilitates the intervention of God. If the psalmist's experience of God is reflected in the abrupt shifts that occur in the lament, grief counseling should be no less open and adaptable to similar abrupt shifts and experiences of intervention. Thus, grief counseling is also nondirective in its pace and timing. While its structure will move through the six stages of the grief experience, the pace with which it moves is determined by the counselee. Just as some psalms of lament vary in length, sometimes this process is relatively brief, other times it is long and tortuous. The important factor is not the duration of the grief process. Pastors used to be advised that the grief should be worked through within three or four months, yet Switzer argues that the normal grief process may last twelve to fifteen months and, in a certain sense, never really end. What *is* important is that, however long the process takes, it follows the pattern of the lament, issuing eventually in an attitude not of frustration, disillusionment, or bitterness, but of genuine praise. The counselee's progress through the stages of the grief experience may occur without any direct efforts by the pastor other than the assurances that I have advocated in the pastoral conversation itself. But if the pastor senses that it is not progressing in this fashion, it is certainly appropriate that the necessary actions be taken to keep the process moving. To say that the basic method in grief counseling is nondirective does not mean that the pastor assumes no responsibility for seeing the process through. Rather, it means that the pastor's role is not to direct the healing process, but to allow spiritual energies to work their will and purpose. This means that the pastor's role is primarily to remove barriers that are impeding a spiritual process.

SUGGESTED PSALMS OF LAMENT

While I have emphasized the use of the lament form in shaping the counseling process itself, this does not preclude using selected psalms in counseling the grieving. The following psalms of personal lament are appropriate for particular experiences of grief. Whether or not they are actually read in the pastoral conversation, they are valuable for clarifying the pastor's thoughts and emotions in the course of caring for individuals with these particular complaints. While these psalms of lament are applicable to the situations indicated, there is no way of knowing whether these are the situations that originally inspired them.

For one who fears that death is imminent: Psalm 6; Psalm 139. In Psalm 6, the lamenter complains that his bones and his soul are troubled, and asks, "How long?" He petitions God to save his life, for "in death there is no remembrance of thee." But his weeping and moaning are heard by God, and his prayer is accepted. In Psalm 139, the lamenter recognizes that God has known him from the very beginning of his life, for "thou didst knit me together in my mother's womb." If this is so, there is no possible way that he could ever be separated from God's supportive presence: "If I take the wings of the morning and dwell in the uttermost parts of the sea, even there thy hand shall lead me, and thy right hand shall hold me." Moreover, even the darkest places are "as light with thee."

For the terminally ill: Psalm 41. The lamenter complains that his enemies are waiting for him to die, and even his most trusted friend no longer cares about him. But he finds he can endure this ill-treatment, because he has acted with integrity and God has set him in his presence forever.

For one who faces an uncertain future: Psalm 42. This lament is appropriate both for the dying and for the bereaved.

The lamenter's complaint focuses on the disquiet of his soul. He longs for a glimpse of God's presence, but his enemies claim that his God has abandoned him. His soul is "cast down" within him," and he asks God, "Why hast thou forgotten me?" Yet, even in the depths of despair, he confesses to his continuing hope in God, and vows to praise God again.

For the bereaved: Psalm 90. The lamenter complains that human life is all too transitory ("the years of our life are threescore and ten"), and even the days we have available to us are filled with toil and trouble. He asks for God's steadfast love, so that his days of affliction will be offset by days of joy and gladness; and he asks God to ensure that at least the *labor* if not the *lives,* of his people will have a degree of permanence.

For those who face premature death: Psalm 102. The lamenter complains that his days pass away like smoke, his bones burn like a furnace, and his heart has withered like the grass—all evidence that God has broken his strength in midcourse and has shortened his days. He asks God to save him from destruction before his appointed time has come, but he is confident that, whatever happens, his children will dwell secure and give God the praise which he, in his present circumstances, has difficulty expressing.

For one who feels threatened in old age: Psalm 71. The lamenter complains that, in his old age, he is the victim of the cruel and the unjust. He petitions God to protect him in his weakness and infirmity, that, even as he protected him in his youth, he will also watch over him in his old age. He expresses confidence that God will increase his honor, provide comfort, and rescue him from those who sought to do him harm.

For one who grieves over a broken relationship: Psalm 55. The lamenter complains that he has been betrayed by his companion and familiar friend, an individual with whom he "used to hold sweet converse together." He wishes he could simply leave the scene of conflict, but knowing that this is impossible, he calls on God to sustain him in the midst of his loneliness and humiliation.

For one who grieves over past mistakes: Psalm 38. The lamenter acknowledges that God was right to chasten him for his past errors, but he feels that he has suffered enough and asks for relief. He claims that he has succeeded in ignoring the threats of his enemies, and the aloofness of his friends and relatives, but he continues to wait for God's assurance that he is "not far" from him.

For one who grieves over loss of personal prestige: Psalm 62. The lamenter is angry that his enemies have succeeded in ruining his career, and that he is no longer treated with respect. But he places his confidence in God and not in dishonest methods of recovering his former status in life. For "power belongs to God" and God does not "requite a man according to his work."

For one who grieves over lack of personal success: Psalm 73. The lamenter confesses that he has allowed envy of those who are successful in life to embitter him. He admits that this has virtually ruined his relationship with God: "When my soul was embittered, when I was pricked in heart, I was stupid and ignorant, I was like a beast toward thee." He now recognizes that the successes of others which so embittered him are not lasting, while his relationship to God is a permanent possession which is all-sufficient. He concludes, "There is nothing upon earth that I desire besides thee."

CONCLUSION

Throughout this chapter, I have focused on grief counseling relating to the death of a loved one. I have emphasized this form of grief counseling because it is the one for which pastors feel a special responsibility. Given their involvement in the funeral and burial service, their counseling of the bereaved is typically an extension of these formal pastoral activities. Most often, the funeral, burial, and related activities initiate the lament process, with pastoral visits and counseling sessions continuing the process. We should view the lament, therefore, as a fluid process, one that is not necessarily confined to the counseling process itself.

We should also emphasize that a single pastoral conversation will rarely include all six stages of the lament. It is most likely that a single conversation will focus on a single stage —especially during the middle stages of the complaint, the petition, and the assurance. Thus, unless the pastor and the parishioner set up a series of conversations, which is not the usual practice of most ministers, the pastor's conversations with a bereaved parishioner are likely to be confined to one or two stages of the lament. This means that the pastor will typically make use of other pastoral initiatives that are available to help the bereaved parishioner work through those stages not covered in one-to-one conversations. With the lament form as a guide, one can usually ascertain the parishioner's current grief state, and can take appropriate initiatives to see that the process is carried through. But this means allowing the bereaved to move step by step, at his own pace.

Psalm 131 issues a valuable instruction in this regard. It says: "O LORD, my heart is not lifted up, my eyes are not raised too high; I do not occupy myself with things too great and too marvelous for me. But I have calmed and quieted my soul." This sense of not overreaching is good for one to keep in mind as one helps the bereaved walk through the grief experience at the person's own pace.

Finally, while I have focused here on the loss of loved ones through physical death, it should be emphasized that the lament form is applicable to other types of grief encountered in pastoral care and counseling. I have taken note of other types of grief in my suggestions of psalms that are appropriate for various experiences of grief, such as loss of professional standing, a broken love relationship, and grief over past mistakes. Thus, the lament form is applicable to the middle-aged parishioner who has lost a job, the college student who has broken an engagement to marry, or the young married person who deeply regrets an irresponsible past. Also, it is often because pastors have known the grief inherent in *ministry* that they are able to help their grieving parishioners make their lonely walk through the valley of the shadow of death.[36]

Chapter 3
The Use of Proverbs
and Premarital Counseling

The proverbs within the Bible represent a treasure of human experience that has claim to divine sanction. The proverbs seek to define the patterns that have been most successful in people's dealings with one another and that have inspired people to seek better lives. They emphasize the importance of norms for guiding human behavior and may be valuable in encouraging moral development. Although the proverbs address many aspects of human relationships, I wish to deal here with their relevance for people who are anticipating marriage.

The present chapter has four main parts. First we will consider Jay Adams' legalistic use of proverbs as the basis of directive moral counseling. Secondly, we will deal with more recent biblical scholarship that reveals the weaknesses of Adams' approach. Then the chapter will move into an alternative approach that will focus on premarital counseling as moral education, emphasizing moral growth and development. On the basis of this discussion we will be able to make some suggestions for premarital counseling centering on moral development, the formation of moral character, and the importance of virtue in a marriage relationship.

BEHAVIORAL CHANGE AND THE PROVERBS

Jay E. Adams' directive, behavior-oriented approach to biblical counseling gives special prominence to the book of Proverbs. In *The Use of the Scriptures in Counseling,* he advises pastors to promote daily Bible-reading by their counselees, and suggests that this program begin with the book of Proverbs. The counselee should start with the list of single proverbs in ch. 10: "In this way he can read through slowly until he strikes a proverb that seems to embody a pithy concept that he needs to grasp and knead into the dough of his life." Adams also lists biblical passages for more than forty personal problems, ranging from adultery to worry, and recommends more passages from Proverbs than from any other biblical text. Let's take a closer look at Adams' views on the role of Proverbs in pastoral conversation.

His clearest discussion of this appears in his book, *Competent io Counsel,* where he develops his view that Proverbs is a book of directive counseling. He says here that counselors find the book of Proverbs so useful because it is a book of "good counsel." Proverbs "anticipates the pitfalls and problems of life and directs the reader to make biblical responses to them. Proverbs capsulizes segments of life as God expects his children to live it in a sinful world."

The key word here is "directs." For, in Adams' view, Proverbs' use of the words "reproof" and "discipline" is nearly synonymous with the word "counsel." So counseling informed by Proverbs should involve direction, reproof, discipline, and recommendations for new ways of behaving. In Adams' view, "Proverbs is anything but non-directive." Instead of allowing counselees to depend on their own insights, counseling based on the proverbs insists that insight comes from others. In Prov. 8:14, Wisdom is personified and made to say, "I have counsel and sound wisdom" and "I have

insight, I have strength." Thus, "Wisdom (as the ideal counselor) gives advice; tells people what to do." In other proverbs, counsel is expressed in the form of paternal advice:
"My son, do not despise the Lord's discipline or be weary of
his reproof, for the Lord reproves him whom he loves, as a
father the son in whom he delights" (3:11–12). Adams concludes, "Plainly the reproof that is spoken of is the kind of
discipline that a father gives to his son for the son's own
benefit." Thus, Proverbs makes clear that "an outside source
imposed upon the counselee from above in an authoritative
fashion by means of precepts, commandments, instruction,
words, reproof, discipline and correction, is what a young
man (or any client seeking counseling) needs. Rather than
encouraging clients to do all of the talking, counselors frequently ought to urge clients to listen to words of advice. The
counselee needs to learn to listen. That he has not done so
in the past, may be one major cause of his present distress."

Adams' view that Proverbs is directive also contrasts feeling and behavior. He criticizes Carl Rogers' emphasis on the
"primacy of feeling," contending that, biblically, behavior is
primary: "People feel bad because of bad behavior; feelings
flow from actions." Thus, bad feelings are a warning that our
actions are bad, and the solution is not to work on one's
feelings but to eradicate the behavior that is responsible for
them. Adams takes exception to Seward Hiltner's view that
"action is no substitute for clarification" and that "most
counseling situations which begin with a wrestle over an
action decision do not get far if they remain only at that level;
if they fail to explore the feelings which lie beneath each
possible action."[37] Adams vigorously disagrees and, in his
judgment, here the line is drawn between client-centered
counseling and his own "nouthetic counseling."

Nouthetic counseling (based on the Greek word "to ad-
monish") "assumes that the feelings are not the most profound level of human relationship with which one must be

concerned in counseling." The Bible speaks of love in behavioral not emotional terms when it defines love as keeping God's commandments. Moreover, feelings cannot be altered directly in the same way that one can change behavior. Consequently, in accordance with Scripture, nouthetic counselors spend less time finding out how people feel. They are more interested in discovering how clients behave." And Proverbs supports this behavioral emphasis because it recognizes that the goal of instruction, reproof, discipline, and correction is "to change behavior for one's benefit."

As Hiltner, Oates, and Wise do not limit themselves to the Psalms, Adams uses biblical passages other than Proverbs. But Proverbs is paradigmatic for Adams because it provides a basic model for pastoral counseling. This model is based, in part, on Proverbs' use of the phrase "my son," which Adams takes to mean approval of a paternal approach to the counselee. It is also based on Proverbs' personification of wisdom, suggesting that the counselor's role is the imparting of wisdom. But Proverbs' major contribution to this model of counseling is its emphasis on disciplining, advising, and reproving. In counseling informed by Proverbs, the counselor's role is clearly directive and hence "anti-Rogerian."

While Adams is the only contemporary author who has given Proverbs a central role in pastoral counseling, we should note that Wayne Oates advocated the use of proverbs, especially for instructional purposes. He lists a number of proverbs that, in his judgment, the pastor will find "therapeutically applicable many times in his counseling ministry." He includes in this list a few proverbial sayings from the Gospels—"Those who are well have no need of a physician, but those who are sick" (Mark 2:17) and "The sabbath was made for man, not man for the sabbath" (Mark 2:27). Thus, Adams is not the only one who has recognized the value of the Proverbs for pastoral counseling. But he is unique in having given Proverbs such central importance. In fact, Oates suggests that proverbs fall into the category of "informal" uses of the Bible in counseling. For Adams, Proverbs defines the counseling process—its methods, objectives, and the counselor-counselee relationship.

PROVERBS IN BIBLICAL SCHOLARSHIP

The Neglect of Proverbs

Adams' polemical style and his tendency to misrepresent the views of those he disagrees with[38] has caused many pastoral counselors to dismiss his ideas. However, Proverbs is important for pastoral counseling. Adams' view of its importance paralleled a resurgence of interest in Proverbs by biblical scholars in the 1970s (the same period in which Adams' "nouthetic" approach to counseling was developed). Biblical scholarship in the 1950s and 1960s paid little attention to Proverbs, largely because it seemed peripheral to the Old Testament's dominant emphasis on salvation history.

In a similar way, client-centered pastoral counseling of the same period paid little attention to Proverbs. Wise's *Psychiatry and the Bible* makes fourteen references to the book of Psalms, only one to the book of Proverbs. The reasons for this neglect of Proverbs are not difficult to see. In the first place, Proverbs' general tone is that of advising, and client-centered counselors at that time wanted to dissociate pastoral counseling from the advice-oriented counseling of the preceding era. To them, giving serious attention to the book of Proverbs would have been counterproductive. In the second place, theologically informed pastoral counselors shared biblical scholars' interest in salvation history. This greatly influenced their theological understanding of pastoral counseling and is still reflected in William Oglesby's *Biblical Themes for Pastoral Care.*

Biblical scholars now recognize that Proverbs and other wisdom literature (Ecclesiastes, Job, and various noncanonical writings) were neglected because they appeared to stand outside this "salvation history" motif. As James Crenshaw points out, "The negative assessment of wisdom arose because it was difficult if not impossible to fit her thought into the reigning theological system. The verdict of G. Ernest Wright represents the dominant position for several decades: 'The difficulty of the wisdom movement was that its theological base and interest were too narrowly fixed; and in this respect Proverbs remains near the pagan source of wisdom in which society and the Divine work in history played no real role.' "[39] Crenshaw claims that it is not the theology of wisdom literature but of salvation history that is too narrow, because it fails to take seriously the canonical books that do not fit the salvation history motif.

Crenshaw cites other important reasons why wisdom literature was neglected. The similarities between Israelite wisdom and that of her pagan environment led scholars, even those who were not wedded to the salvation history theme, to consider wisdom literature devoid of revelatory content: "The international character of wisdom, its universalistic appeal, is here understood as an inherent deficiency." Also, fully half of the extant wisdom literature of ancient Israel (for example, Sirach, Wisdom of Solomon, and IV Maccabees) does not enjoy full canonical status. Since this literature and the canonical books (Proverbs, Job, and Ecclesiastes) are similar in form, vocabulary, and subject matter, the difficulty of "making sharp distinctions between the two bodies of literature resulted in a leveling of the authority granted canonical wisdom."

What accounts for the resurgence of interest in the wisdom literature in the 1970s? In Crenshaw's view, the major reason is that the grounds for an almost exclusive emphasis on salvation history began to erode. "History as the key to an understanding of the theological distinctiveness of ancient Israel has been found lacking, and with this recognition comes renewed appreciation for those texts which offer a universalistic alternative." Accompanying this erosion of the "reigning theological system" based on salvation history was a new "appreciation for the understanding of reality expressed in traditions other than our own, so that wisdom's affinities with Egyptian and Mesopotamian texts has now become an asset rather than a liability." Furthermore, the explosion of Roman Catholic biblical scholarship after Vatican II did much to offset the stigma under which extracanonical wisdom books had suffered in Protestant scholarship.

Since Adams developed his counseling method to help Christians cope with life in "a sinful world," it is ironic that his appeal for the return to biblical counseling is based on texts that biblical scholars ignored until recently because their similarity to the wisdom literature of Israel's "pagan environment" cast doubt on their "revelatory content." It is also ironic that Adams severely criticizes pastoral counseling that is contaminated by worldly psychotherapies when these wisdom texts reflect the universalistic thrust of Israel's religious experience. Given these ironies, we need to ask whether Adams has correctly understood Proverbs. Is his counseling model based on a fundamental misunderstanding of this text? By taking a more careful look at the formal design of Proverbs, we will see that his understanding of Proverbs' significance for pastoral counseling is misguided. In developing a more responsible rationale for Proverbs' use in pastoral counseling, I will focus on the social and religious intentions that are evident in the whole collection of proverbs. In contrast to my discussion of the lament as a unique form within the larger collection of Psalms, I will not focus on a particular type of proverb, but on the whole collection.

Proverbs: Its Basic Structure

The structure of the book of Proverbs can be discussed on two levels. The first concerns the fact that Proverbs is composed of different sections. The second, and most important for our purposes here, concerns its social and religious perspectives.

Regarding the first level, Proverbs consists of five sections. The first section, made up of discourses on wisdom, comprises chs. 1 to 9. As J. Coert Rylaarsdam points out, this section makes clear that the book is primarily intended to build character and standards of conduct in the young, but is also meant for persons of all ages, including those who have already gained considerable wisdom in dealing with life's problems.[40]

The second section, entitled "The Proverbs of Solomon," comprises chs. 10:1 to 22:16. In contrast to the larger discourses in the first section, this section consists entirely of two-line aphorisms, each complete in itself. Rylaarsdam points out that those two-line units are not thematically ordered: "Even when two or more successive proverbs deal more or less with the same subject . . . the connection seems incidental rather than organic. There is no logical continuity of thought." These aphorisms deal with such diverse topics as wisdom and folly, sadness, the poor, self-control, taking bribes, haughtiness and humility, wives, poverty and wealth, and so forth.

The third section, chs. 22:17 to 24:34, consists of thirty sayings, many borrowed from a document of the Egyptian wisdom movement, "The Instruction of Amen-em-opet." Typical sayings dealt with in this section are the obligation to protect the poor, warnings against giving pledges, developing a healthy suspicion of rulers, and the dangers of drunkenness.

The fourth section of Proverbs is chs. 25:1 to 29:27. It bears a prefatory note that its contents are Solomon's proverbs copied by the men of Hezekiah, king of Judah. The first part of this section (25:2 to 27:22) deals with such topics as speaking the right word at the right time, exercising self-control, portraits of a fool and a lazy man, quarreling, scheming, the transiency of life, and proper humility. The second part of this section (28:1 to 29:27) deals with such topics as law and justice, oppression, and disciplining sons and servants.

The fifth section of Proverbs, chs. 30:1 to 31:31, consists of four appendixes, including a brief oracle attributed to a sage named Agur, a series of numerical proverbs ("Three things are too wonderful for me; four I do not understand . . ."), some words of advice taught to the desert king, Lemuel, by his mother, and an acrostic poem on the virtuous wife.

This brief overview of the skeletal structure of Proverbs provides ample evidence that it is "made up of a number of separate collections, each having its own characteristics and its own separate history."[41] Further discussion of the efforts of biblical scholars to reconstruct these separate histories, to ascertain the dates of each collection, and to determine how the book was compiled, would take us too far afield from our primary interests here. But the fact that the book is a compilation of separate collections of proverbial material suggests that we will not be able to gain a clear understanding of its value for pastoral counseling by limiting ourselves to the first level of the book's formal design. Instead, we need to penetrate this skeletal structure and probe the social and religious intentions that lie behind its present shape and form. For this, we turn to Gerhard von Rad's classic work, *Wisdom in Israel.*[42]

Von Rad's View of the Moral Perspective of Proverbs

Von Rad notes the sheer diversity and apparent disunity of the book of Proverbs: "The book of Proverbs presents us ... with a multiplicity of individual realities which are at first difficult to survey. . . . We find particularly aggravating the lack of any order determined by subject-matter, or any arrangements in the collection of sentences and teachings." Occasionally, one finds a group of proverbs in which related material has come together. But, for understanding Proverbs as a whole, "these small ordered arrangements are of no significance, for they appear too sporadically." A further annoying factor is that Proverbs is "the result of the intellectual activity of about eight centuries; only with difficulty, however, could it be arranged chronologically." Confronted with these aggravations, earlier biblical scholars focused on the social circumstances presupposed by this didactic material.

But von Rad argues for a different approach. Instead of beginning with questions about external circumstances presupposed by the literature, a more fruitful approach is to examine its religious world view. The question is not what external circumstances may tell us about the structure of the book, but what unity or order its authors saw in the world. Thus: "It now appears more important and more interesting to examine the proverbs and teachings from the point of view of the intellectual work achieved in them. With what end in view were events examined? What was looked for in them, and what was it hoped to find? If, in fact, something of the nature of an order was recognized, how was it expressed?" This approach enables us to understand that what the proverbs have in common is a concern with "certain basic phenomena which were observed in more or less all spheres of life," and that these observations are expressed "in the style of simple statements, not of exhortations. They simply state what has been experienced."

Von Rad identifies two strategies that the proverbs employ for understanding what has been experienced. He discusses these strategies under the heading "The Essentials for Coping with Reality," indicating that they were originally taught as tools for dealing more effectively with the world. These strategies—the *observation of order* and *cause-effect reasoning*—are designed to identify the order that exists in the world of experience.

Observation of Order

Von Rad acknowledges that there are proverbs in which value judgments are made (e.g., "Better is a dry morsel with quiet than a house full of feasting with strife"). But most are simple statements about how things are ("The poor is disliked even by his neighbor, but the rich has many friends"). This second type of proverb reflects a characteristic attitude of Proverbs toward the world of experience. It takes note of how things are, does not attempt to alter it, but simply advises taking such facts into account in one's engagement with the world: "That the buyer first of all complains about the goods, but that, after the purchase, he boasts (Prov. 20:14), is perhaps funny, but whoever wishes to get to know men must also know about such peculiar types of behavior; some time or another, this knowledge will be of use to him."

These proverbs do not make an appeal to change such conditions. They do not assert that conditions should be altered so that the poor will have as many friends as the rich: "In these sentences, we find ourselves to some extent in a sphere where social appeals are not envisaged at all." But what these proverbs do communicate is the importance of observing "the contradictions in social life and . . . the puzzles which arise within this sphere of tension." Learning to observe such contradictions in social life is important. It is part of the intellectual work involved in examining the world of experience and discovering whatever order it manifests.

The social world is only one sphere of human experience to which such intellectual work is directed. There is also the psychological sphere, or inner life. Here, also, the proverbs are especially aware of the contradictory and puzzling features of human experience: "Even in laughter the heart is sad, and the end of joy is grief" (14:13). Or, "The heart knows its own bitterness, and no stranger shares its joy" (14:10). These proverbs do not attempt to change these peculiarities of the inner life, but knowledge of them helps one cope more effectively with reality. They, too, are part of the order of life.

Proverbs also observe the characteristics and peculiarities of the natural world—animals, wind, the cycles of the year, and so forth. Here such observations are largely analogies of human behavior: "Like clouds and wind without rain is a man who boasts of a gift he does not give" (25:14); "As in water face answers to face, so the mind of man reflects the man" (27:19); "In the light of a king's face there is life, and his favor is like the clouds that bring the spring rain" (16:15). Why the natural world serves as analogies of human behavior rather than the reverse is not difficult to see. In the training of young men for various kinds of public service where they would need to be able to cope with human behavior, known natural phenomena could impart knowledge about the strange mysteries and peculiarities of human relationships. Furthermore, these proverbs about the natural world link two totally different phenomena, and this linking through analogy is itself a gain in knowledge. In effect, linking an affirmation about nature with an affirmation about human behavior results in a third affirmation: "that there is something common to the two affirmations made by the sentence." This third affirmation is a modest but genuine step toward the notion that there is an all-embracing order to life. The worlds of social interaction, of inner experience, and of nature have observable connections. While filled with their contradictions and puzzling features, they share a common order. In fact, "one could almost say that the further apart the subjects being compared lay, the more interesting must the discovery of analogies have been, in so far as this revealed something of the breadth of the order that was discovered."

Proverbs that show analogous relationships between two spheres are the clearest examples of this affirmation of an all-embracing order of life. But von Rad cites two other types of proverbs that support this view of reality. One is based on the observation that something valid in one area of life is valid in a related area: "Sheol and underworld lie open before Yahweh; how much more the hearts of men" (15:11). The other type is the numerical proverb: "Three things are too wonderful for me, and four I do not understand: the way of the eagle in the sky, the way of the serpent on the rock, the way of the ship in the middle of the sea, and the way of a man with a young woman" (30:18–19). In this numerical proverb, the common factor is that all four things are beyond comprehension. Moreover, the human interaction, while closest to hand, is actually the most difficult to understand. Both the comparative and the numerical proverb link two or more spheres of reality and demonstrate commonalities between them, thus contributing to the affirmation of an all-embracing order of life.

Cause-Effect Reasoning

This second strategy also supports affirmation of an all-embracing order. If the previous strategy linked two or more orders of reality, placing them side by side and noting their similarities, this one discerns a natural succession of events. The proverb "Pride goes before destruction, and a haughty spirit before a fall" (16:18) is an example. In discovering the relationship between the destruction and fall and the attitudes that caused them, one has gained insight into the order of life. As von Rad puts it: "Daily, incessantly, man encounters contingent events (chance events) whose meaning and inner necessity are at first hidden from him. Only occasionally does he succeed in recognizing behind the contingent event a clear, inner necessity. Then the contingent loses its contingent character, and its place is taken by the awareness of an order which is at work behind the experiences."

The proverbs give particular attention to cause-effect relationships in the psychological domain of inner experience: "Hope deferred makes the heart sick, but a desire fulfilled is a tree of life" (13:12), or "A glad heart is good for the body, but a broken spirit dries up the bones" (17:22). Also, many proverbs note causal connections in human experience that seem odd or paradoxical. Why is it that a generous person acquires still more, while a stingy person grows poorer? Or why is it that applying the rod to the child can actually benefit the child? Much human experience, when viewed in causal terms, is puzzling and ambiguous. The most instructive instance of this ambiguity is the juxtaposition of two proverbs that contradict each other. The proverb, "Answer not a fool according to his folly, lest you be like him yourself" is followed by the proverb, "Answer a fool according to his folly, lest he be wise in his own eyes" (26:4–6). Biblical scholars agree that this juxtaposition was intentional. In von Rad's view, Proverbs recognizes that "even the most established experiences can be confronted at any time with something that contradicts them." But this does not mean that there is no order in life: "On the contrary, if one faces up to [contradiction] and allows it a place in one's system of knowledge, then behind the paradox, that is, behind the apparent abnormality, a new pattern can be discerned."

The most notable feature of Proverbs' use of cause-effect reasoning is the primacy it gives to *moral order*. Many pro-

verbs make the point that an evil deed has disastrous consequences, while a good deed results in blessing. These proverbs are mainly descriptive. They do not advocate good
deeds, but rather observe that good naturally follows from
good deeds: "Be assured, an evil man will not go unpunished,
but those who are righteous will be delivered"(11:21); "No ill
befalls the righteous, but the wicked are filled with trouble"
(12:21). Such assertions are made objectively, as though they
were stating a proven relationship between cause and effect.
They should therefore not be understood theologically, as if
they were stating a doctrine of retribution. On the contrary,
"these sentences are not concerned with a divine, juridicial
act which subsequently deals out to men blessing or punishment, but with an order of life which can be experienced."

Nor should the modern reader consider such assertions a
naive view of the moral order. Many proverbs acknowledge
that the lot of the righteous is difficult, and others agree that
the blessings of life, such as material wealth, often fail to
bring happiness. But the assumption that good will be rewarded and evil punished is based on "experiences that had
actually been confirmed again and again in a firmly established community," a community that finds evil detrimental
to itself and punishes the perpetrator. In addition, such assurances assume that one must be content to wait for events to
come to their rightful conclusion: "He who rebukes a man
will *afterward* find more favor than he who flatters with his
tongue" (28:23); "An inheritance gotten hastily *in the beginning* will *in the end* not be blessed" (20:21); "A faithful man
will abound with blessings, but he who *hastens* to be rich will
not go unpunished" (28:20). Thus, evidence that the wicked
are prospering and the righteous are struggling does not
mean that there is no moral order to life, but rather that the
"succession of events" precipitated by good or bad behavior
has not yet come to its appointed end: "Let not your heart
envy sinners, but continue in the fear of the Lord all the day.

Surely there is a future, and your hope will not be cut off" (23:17–18).

This confidence in the moral order of life is not a form of quietism. To the wisdom teachers, good is a positive force, and they "took great pains to encourage their pupils to put their trust in this life-promoting force" by committing themselves to a life of wise and righteous behavior. On the other hand, they were not interested in lofty imperatives but in acts of practical wisdom and common virtue. They emphasized the "healing quality of good conduct."

Nor is this confidence in the moral order a pollyannish refusal to recognize evil. To the wisdom teachers, evil is real, but awareness of evil should not cause one to relinquish one's trust in the moral order of life. In von Rad's view, a major achievement of the proverbs as instructional tools was to create trust in the moral order of things; not, though, by advocating or preaching trust, but by marshaling evidence that trust is the appropriate response to the world of human experience. Such trust is clearly supported by the few proverbs that speak explicitly of trust in God and of the advantages of a trusting attitude toward God. But the basic instructional thrust of Proverbs was not to make a general point about the advantages of trusting in God, but to draw attention to "the reality and the evidence of the order which controls the whole of life. . . . This order was, indeed, simply there and could, in the last resort, speak for itself. The fact that it quietly but reliably worked towards a balance in the ceaselessly changing state of human relationships ensured that it was experienced over and over again as a beneficent force."

While Proverbs is concerned with the acquisition of "wisdom," this does not mean "wisdom" in the philosophical sense, but in the moral sense. It means training in moral values, growth in moral character, and commitment to the maintenance of the moral order of life. As we explore the implications of the proverbs for pastoral conversation, their emphasis on moral instruction and the moral order is of focal importance.

Critique of Jay E. Adams' Views of Proverbs

Since Jay E. Adams is largely responsible for noting the value of Proverbs for pastoral counseling, it seems appropriate that we begin our discussion of the role of Proverbs in pastoral conversation by evaluating his views in the light of what we have just learned about Proverbs. Von Rad's analysis of Proverbs supports some aspects of Adams' view of this text. For example, Adams is right to view Proverbs as a book of instruction concerned to help individuals, particularly the young, to live more effective lives. He is also correct in his argument that Proverbs is concerned more with behavior than with feelings. Many proverbs emphasize good actions, and a few stress emotional control. He is also correct in noting that Proverbs speaks positively about discipline and reproof. In these respects, Adams' view of Proverbs is accurate.

But Adams has a distorted view of the moral perspective of Proverbs, and this causes him to misconstrue its *instructional, behavioral,* and *disciplinary* emphases. This distortion is reflected in his statement that Proverbs "capsulizes segments of life as God expects his children to live it in a sinful world." This statement totally misses Proverbs' emphasis on the interconnections of all aspects of life (social, psychological, natural) and its resistance to viewing life in terms of "segments." Also, his suggestion that Proverbs views the world as "sinful" fails to take account of its awareness of the moral order that inheres in the world of experience, and thus fails to pay due regard to the fact that Proverbs supports a confident engagement in the world, not a fear of being corrupted by it.

This misunderstanding of the overall moral perspective of Proverbs leads Adams to misrepresent its views of instruction, behavior, and discipline. While Proverbs is *instructional,* its instructional method does not support a counseling model in which "an outside source [is] imposed upon the counselee from above in an authoritative fashion." Von Rad makes clear that the proverbs do not appeal to the authority of the teacher or even to the authority of God. Rather, the authoritativeness of the proverbs is based on the accuracy of their observations of the world of experience. This does not mean, of course, that the wisdom teachers gave their pupils license to reject their teachings. But to say that they "imposed" their teachings on their pupils misses the fact that the proverbs make their appeal on their own merits. They are persuasive because they give a true account of human experience.

Concerning Adams' view that Proverbs is *behavior-oriented,* the authors of Proverbs do stress the importance of behavior and criticize individuals who give primacy to the emotions. But Proverbs is also concerned with a person's inner experience. Various proverbs reflect sensitivity to the feelings of the heart: "Hope deferred makes the heart sick, but a desire fulfilled is a tree of life" (13:12). Proverbs makes a moral distinction between emotions and feelings. Giving vent to rash emotions, such as outbursts of anger or violent language, is condemned. But expression of deep inner feelings—such as sorrow, joy, delight, and affection—is approved. The one leads to bad conduct, the other gives rise to good conduct. In addition, inner psychological experience is not subordinated to the social or natural spheres, but is just as carefully cultivated as these "external" areas of human experience. This cultivation means probing the connections between inner psychological experience and the external world of human actions: "*Anxiety* in a man's heart weighs him down, but a *good word* makes him glad" (12:25).

Concerning Adams' view that a major theme of Proverbs is *discipline,* there are in fact a number of proverbs about the use of the rod. And there is no question that these proverbs make some biblical scholars uneasy. Rylaarsdam hopes that the author who advocated the use of corporal punishment of children (23:13–14) also shares the sentiment of the following verses in which the teacher rejoices over his student. If so, any "evil effects" of the corporal punishment "might perhaps be deflected." And, concerning the proverbs in 29:15 and 17, which advocate the use of the rod, he observes that "corporal punishment of sons and pupils in Israel was coupled with great love and devotion toward them. This probably reduced the harm it did." Thus, when these proverbs are viewed within the larger moral perspective of the book of Proverbs, discipline is tempered with love, justice with mercy.

This issue of discipline may also be viewed in terms of Proverbs' strategies of observation of life's order and cause-effect reasoning. The basic issue is not whether Proverbs prescribes a certain form of child-rearing that we should continue to enforce today. If this were so, we should be as zealous in carrying out the mandate of 29:19 (which advocates using the rod on slaves) or even 26:3 (which says: "A whip for the horse, a bridle for the ass, and a rod for the back of fools"). Rather, the issue is that observation of these disciplinary procedures reveals a fundamental truth. Behavior that seems "bad" for the relationship of parent and child actually helps to establish "good" relationships between them. Proverbs dealing with many other themes besides disciplining children note this same fundamental paradox in the moral order of life. If you rebuke a person, you will not necessarily incur this person's disfavor (28:23). If a friend hurts you, this may be a sign of his faithfulness (27:6). Proverbs about disciplining children with the rod relate to this commonly observed paradox of human experience. They tell us that, in such cases, we should not be too hasty in assessing the ultimate moral effects of a certain behavior. This long-term relationship of cause and effect is the point, after all, of the related proverb, "Train up a child in the way he should go, and when he is old he will not depart from it" (22:6).

This is not to minimize the importance of disciplining children, nor is it an argument for parental leniency. The important issue for our purposes here is not child discipline as such but Adams' use of these proverbs to differentiate his own counseling theory from client-centered counseling. The differences between nondirective and directive pastoral counseling are real and well worth discussing from biblical perspectives, but these proverbs do not provide the clearcut support for directive counseling that Adams thinks they do. Moreover, by focusing his attention on this disciplinary issue, he fails to take note of the much more fundamental moral vision of the book of Proverbs, its conviction that a unifying moral order inheres in the world of human experience. Instead of centering one's attention on reproof and advice-giving, one needs to ask what are the implications of this fundamental moral perspective for pastoral counseling. How might it inform the counseling process?

A FRESH APPROACH TO PREMARITAL COUNSELING THROUGH PROVERBS

Premarital Counseling as Moral Education

Experts in pastoral counseling generally agree that premarital counseling is educational. Charles William Stewart writes: "In one sense premarital counseling is not really counseling; it is teaching. . . . We are taking the position that the minister is dealing here with the education of a couple regarding marriage and family relations and not with specific problems as in personal counseling."[43] Howard J. Clinebell, Jr., discusses premarital counseling in a chapter on "educative" forms of pastoral counseling, noting that educative counseling requires "a blending of the skills of creative education and dynamic counseling."[44] Explaining his view that premarital counseling is educative, Clinebell points out that premarital counseling is usually entered into on the recommendation or insistence of the pastor. Because the counselor takes the initiative, the counseling sessions are more "directive" than they might otherwise be, and this normally means a predetermined agenda, including topics that the counselor considers important to discuss even if the counselees do not. Thus, since premarital counseling is educative, it has the same general objective as Proverbs, to provide instruction.

But instruction for what? For Clinebell, it is instruction for more effective coping. Thus, like Proverbs, premarital counseling "goes far beyond merely imparting information. By utilizing counseling skills and sensitivities, it helps the person understand, evaluate, and then apply the information that is relevant to constructive coping with his particular life situation." We have seen how Proverbs is concerned with various spheres of human experience, including spheres of human interaction and inner experience, and with their interrelationships. These concerns are also important to premarital counseling. It is concerned with how the couple relate to each other and to persons who will be directly affected by the marriage (such as in-laws and children by a previous marriage). It is also concerned with the two persons' inner experience, their feelings toward each other and about themselves. Like Proverbs, good premarital counseling is aware that these two spheres of the couple's lives are inextricably linked. Inner experience and interpersonal relationships influence one another in complex and interesting ways, and being aware of how they interrelate helps one cope more effectively with the situation.

But the major similarity between Proverbs and premarital counseling is that both are engaged in moral education. Pastors whose premarital counseling helps couples identify areas of potential interpersonal conflict or develop better communication skills do not normally consider themselves to be engaged in "moral education." But these typical objectives of contemporary premarital counseling fall under the heading of moral education because they are based on implicit moral assumptions about what makes for a "good" marriage relationship. Furthermore, pastors whose premarital counseling includes careful assessment of the couple's decision to marry are also acting on implicit moral assumptions. Robert F. Stahmann and William J. Hiebert point out that there are two myths about marriage that are commonly held today.[45] One myth is the popular idea that mate selection is merely a matter of chance and therefore one's decision to marry this particular person need not be critically evaluated. The other myth is that marriage is a one-sided relationship, thus a losing proposition for one partner. The pastor who believes that premarital counseling is not a mere formality, but is a critically important opportunity to assess the couple's decision to marry each other, is implicitly rejecting the moral fatalism of these two common myths. He is affirming that mate selection is not a matter of chance, but a choice for which they must both assume responsibility. He is also saying that marital unhappiness is not preordained or inevitable, and that marriage ought not be entered into if one partner has such low expectations of the marriage relationship.

Thus, the premarital counseling practice of many pastors reflects implicit moral assumptions. Unfortunately, the brevity of much premarital counseling and the desire of many ministers to avoid a "paternalistic" or "maternalistic" attitude toward young couples have tended to work against the conscious recognition that premarital counseling is "moral education." Furthermore, even among pastors who have viewed premarital counseling in terms of moral education, this has often involved a rather narrow and stereotypical set of moral "issues." One minister, for example, described marriage as a three-legged stool, with sex, money, and religion each representing one leg of the stool. His "moral education" approach, therefore, focused only on matters of sexual adjustment, budget planning, and church attendance.[46]

In a sophisticated version of the three-legged stool approach, Charles William Stewart advocates devoting the first session of premarital counseling to sexual issues, the second to discussion of the couple's proposed financial budget, and the third to personality differences, religious attitudes, and wedding planning. Stewart contends that the discussion of the budget in the second session "is a particularly good tool to bring out the values by which the couple plan to live when married. Sometimes these values are hidden or assumed; and this honest talk brings them out in the open where they can be seen and worked through with each other."[47] As the budget discussion develops, the pastor finds it natural to ask such questions as: "What standard of living have you been used to in living with your parents or on your own income?" "Who gets what and by what plan? Will you use the dole, the family treasurer, a division of spending responsibilities, a budget, or a joint expense account?" "Do you plan to be employed outside the home after the marriage? If so, for how long? How will this affect your budget? your having children?"

While this budget-planning session may reveal some of the couple's fundamental values, eliciting these values in the course of working out a budget means that they are discussed in terms of their economic implications. Financial security is, of course, an important factor in marital success or failure. Moreover, some couples feel that their finances are the most pressing issue confronting them, and welcome an extended discussion of budgetary matters. Still, Stewart's model reflects the tendency of much premarital counseling to focus on a rather narrow and stereotypical range of moral "issues." In this case, the pastor does not view the woman's vocational aspirations as values in themselves, but asks instead whether she will be employed outside the home and how this will affect the budget.

In my judgment, Proverbs provides the premarital counselor with a more expansive moral perspective than is reflected in much premarital counseling today. Instead of being oriented around one or two "problem" areas, and having all other matters of value and commitment reduced to these issues, Proverbs offers a larger moral perspective that is centered on *moral development* and the *formation of moral character.* I want to turn next to the formulation of this moral perspective in premarital counseling.

The Moral Perspective of Proverbs

Hardly anyone would disagree that the modern couple is confronted with moral decisions never envisioned by the authors of Proverbs. Proverbs offers no advice about ideal family size, about interfaith and interracial marriages, about two-career families, about the couple's mutual rights, or about whether the woman has any rights at all![48] True, Proverbs does deal with a variety of moral issues that confront the recently married couple. Some involve the more obvious moral issues relating to marital fidelity and child discipline. Others deal with more subtle issues, such as appropriate ways of expressing feelings ("Better is open rebuke than hidden love"), resisting the urge to get even ("Do not say, 'I will do to him as he has done to me' "), and being attentive to the emotional needs and desires of the other ("Hope deferred makes the heart sick, but a desire fulfilled is a tree of life" and "He who sings songs to a heavy heart is like one who takes off a garment on a cold day"). But, even if these particular proverbs are applicable to modern premarital counseling, the issue is not that Proverbs addresses the specific moral problems and decisions facing the recently married couple. Rather, the important point is that Proverbs has a moral perspective that is capable of informing the counseling process itself.

This claim that Proverbs offers a moral perspective for modern premarital counseling means three things:

First, it means taking seriously Proverbs' *confidence in the moral order of life,* and making certain that one's premarital counseling reflects this confidence. This dimension of Proverbs' moral perspective is best reflected in its emphasis on *observation of experience* and *cause-effect reasoning.* To many pastors, the main objective of premarital counseling is to alert the couple to the problems they will be confronted with. These pastors want the couple to view married life in a "realistic" way. To that end, they make certain that their counselees are warned of the typical pitfalls that could undermine their marriage, such as poor financial habits, sexual incompatibility, alcohol abuse, meddling in-laws, and the like. Such warnings have their value, but Proverbs' moral perspective reflects greater *confidence* in the moral order of life. As we have seen, this is not a pollyannish refusal to face reality, nor is it a denial that evil exists in the world and in ourselves. It is based on the conviction that moral behavior will make a real difference in the world of human experience. Thus, premarital counseling based on Proverbs' moral perspective takes the more positive approach of helping the couple envision the joys and blessings that result from making significant moral commitments to each other, whether this means pledging to be faithful to each other, committing themselves to the achievement of each other's vocational objectives, reaching out in goodwill to in-laws, or developing capacities for intimacy and caring.

This too is a "realistic" view of marriage, based on observation of human experience. For it is a matter of common observation that virtuous actions are life-promoting; their blessings are self-generated ones. Of course, the couple will experience difficult, perhaps even insoluble problems in the future. But this does not mean that the premarital counseling sessions need to dwell on the problems a couple will typically confront in marriage. There is a theme in Proverbs' moral perspective that von Rad calls the "doctrine of the proper time." This doctrine is reflected in such proverbs as "A word in season, how good it is" (15:23); "Golden apples in silver ornaments, a word spoken at the right time" (25:11); and the violation of this doctrine in the proverb, "He who sings songs to a heavy heart is like one who takes off a garment on a cold day" (25:20). When this doctrine is applied to premarital counseling, we can say that what is proper *now* is not a dire litany of the problems the couple will face in the future, but a well-focused exploration into their moral commitments to each other, together with assurances of the blessings that accompany wise and good conduct. When specific problems emerge in the months or years ahead, it will be proper *at that time* for the pastor to explore these problems with them. But, for now, the task is to help the couple discern the grounds on which their confidence in the moral order of life will be based, and to help them identify the commitments and responsibilities that such confidence will entail, not leaving these matters to chance or fate.

This may well include focusing on specific moral issues, not, however, on "typical" problems that all couples anticipating marriage will "typically" face. Rather, it means centering on matters of moral commitment which are of primary importance to this particular couple. Will Carl support Mary's vocational aspirations? Is Sandy prepared to treat Steve's feelings about his aged mother with understanding and respect? Are Sam and Betty thinking wisely about having and caring for children? The pastor could look at these as potential "problem" areas. But in premarital counseling informed by the moral perspective of Proverbs they are opportunities for evoking or reinforcing the couple's confidence in the moral order of life. This confidence can be built through the premarital counseling process by strengthening moral commitment in those areas of greatest concern to the individual couple.

Second, the moral perspective of Proverbs draws special attention to the importance of *moral development and the formation of moral* character. Given their interest in moral development and the formation of moral character, the work of religious educators in these areas is a valuable resource for premarital counseling. Significantly, Howard Clinebell views educative counseling as "a helping process which integrates the insights and methods of two pastoral functions [religious education and pastoral counseling] with the single objective of fostering the growth of persons."[49] By employing religious educators' work in moral development and character formation in premarital counseling, we can integrate the insights and methods of these two pastoral functions. Particularly valuable in this regard are their use of stage theories of human and moral development, especially those of Erik H. Erikson, Lawrence Kohlberg, and of Robert Peck and Robert Havighurst. Later, I will offer some concrete suggestions for the use of this material in premarital counseling. At this point, I simply want to note the importance of this particular aspect of Proverbs' moral perspective for premarital counseling.

Third, the moral perspective of Proverbs draws attention to the *moral responsibility of the one who is charged with moral education.* Pastors today are increasingly conscious of the fact that their premarital counseling is an area of ministry that carries a moral responsibility. Given the increasing rate of broken marriages in recent years, premarital counseling is one area of ministry in which the pastor's sense of moral responsibility is heightened. Many pastors confess that they have performed marriages that they ought not to have performed. Increasing numbers of pastors are reexamining their premarital counseling methods. But, wary of their predecessors' abuses of their moral authority, many pastors continue to deprive themselves of the opportunities afforded by premarital counseling to be moral educators. As a result of their abdication of their appropriate role as moral educators, their premarital counseling lacks a sense of moral purpose. It focuses primarily on personality and communication issues, and rarely touches on matters of moral commitment and formation. True, premarital counseling that focuses on personality adjustment and communication skills has its own implicit moral assumptions, so I am not about to charge that such counseling lacks moral intent. But exploration of these issues needs to be seen as a part of the overall objective of premarital counseling, the formation of the moral foundations of the marriage relationship.

To be sure, this objective is the task of a lifetime. It cannot be accomplished in the course of two or three premarital counseling sessions. If research on individual moral development can be applied to the marriage relationship, it suggests that development of the marriage relationship, morally speaking, is not a steady growth process that can be easily programmed, but occurs in discrete stages, each reflecting a new plateau of moral awareness. It is unrealistic to assume that two or three premarital counseling sessions will result in movement to a higher moral plateau, or that the "crisis" of approaching marriage will accelerate such movement. Still, moral education for marriage needs to begin somewhere, and premarital counseling affords an excellent opportunity for initiating this process.

This does not mean, of course, that pastors who have tended to abdicate their role as moral educators should go to the opposite extreme of adopting an authoritarian demeanor, imposing their cherished moral insights and gems of moral wisdom on the couple. We must reject Adams' suggestion that, because Proverbs personifies Wisdom, this gives the pastor license to view himself as the dispenser of moral wisdom. Rather, the task is to infuse the counseling process with the moral perspective of Proverbs, with its confidence that those who relate to one another and to others in wisdom and virtue will know life's blessings. As moral educator, the pastor needs to have a basic trust in the moral order of life. He or she needs to be able to assure the couple, with conviction, that they will know life's deep and enduring blessings if they treat each other wisely and virtuously. True, such trust in the moral order of life is not always easy to come by; even, perhaps especially, for ministers of the gospel. While some ministers have insulated themselves from evidence that challenges such trust, and others have trivialized it into a pollyannish optimism, there are many others who achieve such confidence only through a heroic "suspension of disbelief." The difficulty of maintaining such confidence should not be minimized. Nonetheless, when the pastor fails to reflect genuine confidence in the moral order of life, the result is either an abdication of the role of moral educator or a tendency to view this role in an authoritarian, legalistic way.

What of the pastor who has abdicated this role? Can it be recovered? Many pastors have never felt that their role in premarital counseling is to offer advice and admonition. They doubt that the couple would listen to them anyway, or they question whether their own marital experiences would qualify them to offer such words of advice. (Here I have in mind not only those ministers whose marriages are in trouble but also those ministers whose marital experience is limited.) But this need not mean that these pastors are ill equipped to offer moral instruction. As the proverbs show, most moral instruction takes the form of simply observing what is the case in human experience. It is not necessary that one revert to advice and admonition in carrying out one's role as moral educator. Even proverbs that make value judgments are expressed in relative ways: *"Better* is a dry morsel with quiet than a house full of feasting with strife." The reader who responds to this proverb with the wry comment, "assuming these are the only alternatives," catches the relative spirit of the proverb. In a sense, the pastor's role as moral educator in premarital counseling is similar to Martin Luther King Jr.'s role as moral educator in civil rights issues. It is not a matter of offering moral injunctions, but of seeking "the more excellent way" based on observation of the situation and available resources.

What of pastors who have adopted an authoritarian, legalistic approach to premarital counseling? Those who inform the couple about God's moral laws and warn them not to violate these laws, or those who view marriage as a veritable moral minefield which the couple will need to traverse as gingerly as possible lest their marriage end in destruction? To them, the rising divorce rate legitimates this authoritarian approach. However, assessment of the historical evolution of wisdom literature calls this understanding of premarital counseling into serious question. Rylaarsdam points out that the *early* and canonical wisdom books (Proverbs, Ecclesiastes, and Job) used *human experience* as the basis for their moral perspective. The authors of Proverbs recognized that a proverb would be persuasive only if based on accurate observation of human experience. But later writers and non-canonical wisdom writers (Sirach, Baruch, and IV Maccabees) forged a link between wisdom literature and law, contending that the "accumulated lore of human experience must all be brought under the law's jurisdiction." Now the test of the truth of a wisdom statement was no longer its observability in human experience, but its compatability with the *law.* [50]

An "authoritarian" approach in premarital counseling reflects this later development in the historical evolution of wisdom literature. Jay Adams represents this approach when he superimposes this later link between wisdom literature and law on the book of Proverbs. He views Proverbs as Divine Wisdom that provides *laws* for living, and like those in ancient Israel who argued for the completeness of the law, he says that there is no moral question that does not have its answer somewhere in the Scriptures. This legalistic view of Proverbs needs to be resisted. We need to focus, instead, on the fact that Proverbs places confidence and trust in the moral order of *human experience* itself. In later wisdom writers, this confidence in observation of human experience was largely replaced by confidence in the law. Under this view, earlier wisdom literature, including Proverbs, came to be seen as transcendent truths to which individuals are expected to surrender their freedom of action and judgment. When this view is adopted, Proverbs is no longer a collection of astute observations about human experience—observations that give rise to confidence in the moral order of things —but a set of universal rules.[51]

There is strong support for Proverbs' more traditional view of morality in Erik H. Erikson's observations of mother-child relationships. Erikson has shown that trust in the moral order of things is mediated through interaction with parents, teachers, and other human sources of wisdom and virtue, and that such *trust* is the first decisive stage in the formation of moral character.[52] He has also pointed out that, if an individual's appreciation of human and divine law is to be genuinely moral and not merely legalistic, it must be founded on this fundamental trust in the moral order of human experience. As the authors of Proverbs clearly understood, moral character is formed not through imposition of transcendent laws, but through interaction with wise and virtuous persons. Thus, to say that Proverbs provides a set of rules and laws violates its own understanding of how moral growth occurs, that is, through wise and virtuous human interaction.

This interaction is, of course, what the marriage relationship itself can offer. Proverbs does not speak directly about the marriage relationship as a contributor to the moral order of things; though it has much to say about the moral qualities that young men should look for in a wife, it gives little attention to the marriage relationship itself. Still, in empha-sizing the home as a moral universe, and recognizing that the home has potential for either positive or destructive human relationships, it includes family relationships in the formation of our confidence in the moral order.

In short, when the moral perspective of Proverbs informs premarital counseling, the role of the pastor is neither to *abdicate* the position of moral educator nor to adopt an *authoritarian* posture, but to provide *assurance.* Not assurance that all will go well with the couple, that their future will be free of trouble and conflict, but assurance that they can face the future with confidence because their intention to establish their marriage relationship on a firm moral foundation will be richly rewarded.

In cases where this intention is clearly lacking, the pastor's role as moral educator is not to give such assurance with fingers crossed, thus consorting with the pseudo wisdom of chance and fatalistic thinking, but to explain to the couple why it is difficult, in good conscience, to recommend their marriage at this time. This, of course, is one of the most difficult situations that a pastor confronts as moral educator. But to be a moral educator is to be confronted with difficult moral judgments. This is not done in an authoritarian manner, an absolute refusal to marry the couple at any time, but in the spirit of Proverbs' observation of human experience and of cause-effect relationships. It means informing the couple that, *on the basis of what one sees,* the prospects for this marriage are doubtful at this time because the necessary moral commitment *appears* to be absent or weak. The pastor does not need to appeal to any higher authority than the empirical observation that marriages in which one or both partners cannot or will not establish their relationship on a firm moral foundation (cause) are not likely to do well (effect). The pastor who rejects the conventional wisdom that this approach is either punitive or unrealistic shares Proverbs' confidence in the moral order—in this case, the confidence that good counseling will itself be richly rewarded.

SOME CONCRETE SUGGESTIONS

I now want to make some concrete suggestions for use in premarital counseling. These suggestions build on the views developed in the preceding discussion. They are based on the assumption that premarital counseling is a form of educative counseling, and that, as Clinebell points out, the basic method of premarital counseling is directive. It is directive, however, not in an authoritative sense (Adams) but more in an interrogative sense (Stewart), through the use of leading questions. This interrogative approach is quite consistent with the instructional methods of the wisdom teachers of ancient Israel. According to some biblical scholars, they would recite the first line of a proverb and their pupils would make up the second line, a procedure that could account for the fact that there are proverbs with nearly identical first lines but rather different, even conflicting second lines. This "give-and-take" between teacher and pupil serves as a model of directive premarital counseling. The pastor takes the lead in posing issues and raising questions, while the couple supplies the "second line" in a truly collaborative effort.

The concrete suggestions that I propose here are also based on the rather broad agreement among many authorities that, ideally, premarital counseling should consist of three sessions, scheduled one week apart. There are exceptions to this ideal, but three sessions usually allow adequate time to deal with wedding arrangements as well as to lay the foundations for a morally grounded marriage. These sessions need not be limited to one-hour blocks of time. As Stahmann and Hiebert point out, premarital counseling is less likely than other types of counseling to be restricted to the one-hour (or fifty-minute) time frame. They themselves advocate a two-hour session. But the length of each session depends on the circumstances of each individual couple.

The following suggestions do not provide a complete premarital counseling program or a plan for each of the three sessions. They are merely intended as ideas that may be incorporated into such a program, adapted to the particular needs and interests of the individual pastor. I introduce these ideas under three major headings: moral development concerns, moral character concerns, and personal virtue concerns.

Moral Development Concerns

One important facet of the moral life is the process of moral development. In recent years, Lawrence Kohlberg's stage theory of moral development has received considerable attention in religious education. A few pastoral counselors have made use of it in their diagnostic work, but it has not been used to any significant extent in premarital counseling. If used judiciously, it can be a valuable aid in premarital counseling.

In his theory of moral development, Kohlberg identifies six stages of moral reasoning, each more advanced than the preceding one. In order, they focus on *obedience to authority, expectations of fairness based on role expectations and procedures, conformity to social expectation, support of social laws and civic responsibility, universal ethical principles,* and *a moral vision of love, mercy, and justice.* [53] Kohlberg and his associates have expanded his theory in recent years to include other dimensions of moral growth besides moral reasoning. These extensions of the theory are largely centered on the formation of an individual's social perspective and system of values. The theory has also been applied to stages of faith development.[54]

In proposing the use of this theory in premarital counseling, I naturally assume that it is not only applicable to the moral development of the child. It also applies to adults. While older children are capable of stage 5 moral reasoning, very few adults go beyond this stage. Actually, the moral reasoning of the majority of adults centers around stages 3 and 4. Thus, except in the case of younger children, one's moral reasoning has no identifiable relationship to chronological age, and this means that in premarital counseling with adults, the pastor will not encounter only the highest stages of moral reasoning. In fact, given the rarity of stage 6 moral reasoning, and the rather low percentage of adults who reflect stage 5 reasoning, the pastor is most likely to encounter various combinations of stages 2, 3, and 4 in premarital counseling.

The question, then, is not whether Kohlberg's theory is valid for premarital counseling with adults, but how it might be used in premarital counseling. One obvious approach is to have the couple fill out a standardized test designed to determine their level of moral reasoning. James Rest has developed such a test, called the Defining Issues Test (DIT), based on Kohlberg's stages of moral reasoning.[55] But, in my judgment, a better approach is to adapt Kohlberg's original research method to the premarital counseling setting. This method involved guided interviews based on hypothetical stories involving "moral dilemmas" (for example, the only way the husband of a woman dying of cancer can obtain the drug that might save her life is by stealing it). Kohlberg's "moral dilemmas" approach in his research has been adapted for use in religious education, with religious educators using his own stories, stories prepared by others for use with his theories, biblical stories that have moral implications, and situations that occur in the classroom.

For premarital counseling, the most natural and effective approach is to use the couple's own moral dilemmas. Since premarital counseling normally includes conversation about the history of the couple's relationship (how they met, how long they went together before becoming engaged and so forth),[56] this provides an excellent opportunity for exploration of one or two moral dilemmas that were experienced and worked through in the past, or remain unresolved at this time. The pastor ought not to propose "typical" moral dilemmas experienced by engaged couples. Rather, these should be matters that the couple have experienced as real dilemmas in their developing relationship. These may range from their decision to move in with Bill's parents, Mary's heavy financial indebtedness due to previous credit card purchases, Bill's promise to reduce his alcohol consumption, Bill's resistance to Mary's desire to work for a master's degree, Bill's reluctance to tell Mary all about a previous romance, and so forth. Most couples already anticipate that the premarital counseling sessions will involve some exploration of such moral dilemmas, and most feel that such exploration is relevant to the basic purposes of premarital counseling as they understand them, so there is a certain naturalness about this adaptation of Kohlberg's work to the premarital counseling process.

How does this exploration proceed? What does the pastor try to accomplish in this exploration? The procedure that Kohlberg uses to determine an individual's level of moral reasoning may also guide the pastor's exploration of the counselees' moral dilemmas. This procedure involves the following four steps:

1. *Identify the decision.* Since moral dilemmas normally confront an individual (or, in this case, the couple) with a decision, it is important to identify just what that decision

was (if the dilemma was in the past). If the couple are still wrestling with the dilemma, it is important to clarify their current understanding of the decision that will need to be made in the future.

2. *Identify the norm.* When a person makes a moral decision, he or she typically brings in another issue to support it. This is usually a spontaneous application of a "norm" for supporting or justifying the decision. The major themes of the six stages of Kohlberg's theory (obedience to authority; expectations of fairness; conformity to social expectation; support of social laws and civic responsibility; universal ethical principles; moral vision of love, mercy, and justice) provide the pastor with the types of norms that are commonly used in moral decision-making. However, the person who is making the decision does not normally act on a self-conscious selection of a general norm ("I wanted to conform to what was socially expected of me"), but on a concrete application of the norm ("I knew my mother would approve, and that's what I was mainly concerned about"). In premarital counseling, the pastor's task is to identify the norms employed by both persons and to help the couple assess the compatibility or incompatibility of their norms.

3. *Identify modes of decision-making.* When faced with a moral dilemma, individuals use various strategies to help them come to a decision. Kohlberg proposes four strategies that are used in making moral decisions. These include: *(a)* using standards or rules; *(b)* looking at the consequences or results of the decision; *(c)* considering what is fair and just for the persons involved; *(d)* considering what a good person would do in terms of obeying one's conscience, maintaining self-respect, or living up to moral law. Here, again, the pastor will want to be especially attentive to the compatibility between the couple's decision-making strategies. Are the ways they go about solving moral problems rather similar, or are they quite different? If the moral dilemma is Bill's drinking

habits, Mary might apply a rule ("I told Bill he could have one six pack of beer per week. Period"), while Bill might invoke the principle of fairness ("I thought Mary was being pretty legalistic there. It meant there was one day a week I'd have to go without. That didn't seem fair").

4. *Identify social perspective.* How a person arrives at a moral decision has much to do with how he interprets the world of persons and society. What is his social perspective? Synthesizing the work of Kohlberg and his associates, Mary Wilcox identifies six factors of social perspective that are directly relevant to moral thought and action. They include the individual's *(a) concept of persons,* especially how they relate to one another and to society; *(b) concept of the value of human life; (c) role-taking ability,* or how well the person is able to place himself or herself in the shoes of another person and interpret the thoughts and feelings of the other; *(d) concept of authority,* especially its locus, how it functions, and how one relates to it; *(e) concept of law,* including its function and purposes; and *(f) concept of community,* particularly the structures of society and how persons relate to these. The pastor would have considerable difficulty taking all these factors into account in premarital counseling. Wilcox herself places considerable emphasis on the importance of role-taking ability in her work in religious education.[57] This dimension of an individual's social perspective is also important in premarital counseling because the couple's role-taking ability is a major factor in their effectiveness in handling the moral dilemmas encountered in the marriage relationship. The pastor can assess each individual's role-taking ability by asking: What is its *depth,* and what is its *range?* In terms of *depth,* role-taking ability involves a capacity to internalize the thoughts and feelings of the other, not merely to appreciate the reasons why the other acted as he or she did, but to "feel" the other person's inner thoughts and feelings. In terms of *range,* the question is how widely one is able to

cast the role-taking net. Does it include one's future mate's family, friends, ethnic identification, occupational group, religious affiliation?

While an exploration of the couple's moral dilemma includes these four steps, they need not be followed in any rigid fashion. They should be thought of as guidelines that are useful in structuring the pastoral conversation about a moral dilemma, and for lifting out some of the more noteworthy features of this episode or event. To illustrate how this may work, let's consider the following excerpt from a premarital counseling case.[58] This is the moral dilemma: Valerie and Bill plan to move into Bill's apartment after they are married and they have agreed that Bill's roommate, Harry, will not be asked to move out. The pastor has some serious reservations about this arrangement, and asks what plans have been made for sharing the work load and for payment of the rent:

PASTOR: Who is going to wash the dishes, wash clothes, vacuum and keep the apartment clean?

BILL: We will all share the work—Valerie, Harry, and I. Besides, we have a dishwasher and the apartment is easy to keep clean.

VALERIE: I will probably end up doing most of the work. Yes, my mother warned me about the same thing you are saying, but I can handle it and I don't think I will mind.

PASTOR: How will Harry feel about living with you two, and how will you share your expenses so that it will be fair for the three of you?

BILL: Harry has agreed that we can divide the rent into three parts.

VALERIE: You did not tell me that. I don't think it

	is fair. Maybe we can pay a little over the half but not two thirds.
BILL:	You shut up, you don't know what you're talking about.
PASTOR:	Bill, I thought you said a while ago that both of you would be equal in rights and in decisions.
BILL:	Well, I was just kidding.
VALERIE:	No, you weren't (said firmly, yet smiling).

This is clearly a moral dilemma that has not yet been resolved. Bill and Valerie agreed together that they would share the apartment with Harry, and Valerie, perhaps operating on the myth that marriage is inevitably a one-sided proposition, is reconciled to the prospect that she will probably have to do most of the work. But Bill has entered into a financial arrangement with Harry without first consulting with Valerie, and this action creates the "moral dilemma." Should he have done this without consulting with her? The first stage of *decision-making* has not yet been finalized. Instead, it is being worked through in the counseling process itself.

In questioning Bill's action, Valerie uses one norm and Bill uses another. She uses the norm of *expectations of fairness,* not in relation to herself but procedurally. In his response to her proposal for a more equitable financial arrangement with Harry, Bill resorts to a norm of *obedience to authority:* "You shut up, you don't know what you're talking about," which is to say, "I know what's best, so don't question it." This incompatibility in norms should be of concern to the pastor, especially since Bill employs a stage 1 norm.

Next, we look at the *strategy* employed in resolving the dilemma. Now that Bill's arrangement with Harry has come to light and a moral dilemma is apparent, he reveals that he does what is fair for all concerned only when he finds it convenient. Valerie challenges him on this, as does the pastor, but neither pursues it very far. No real strategy is developed for resolving the dilemma. Evidently, Bill will be allowed to have his own way. He exhibits no interest in considering the merits of Valerie's proposal for a more equitable arrangement with Harry, does not acknowledge that he should have consulted with her about the arrangement, and feels no obligation now to consider her counterproposal.

As to *role-taking* ability, Bill does not exhibit any ability to see the situation from Valerie's point of view. He does not consider her thoughts and feelings in the matter but informs her, in no uncertain terms, that her thoughts and feelings are not worth considering. In contrast, Valerie seems to have these role-taking abilities. Even though she does not agree with her mother and pastor, she can appreciate what they are saying to her. She also seems to be able to understand Bill's feelings (for example, she rejects Bill's evasive "Well, I was just kidding" because she believes that this does not reflect his true feelings about their equality in rights and decision-making).

In short, there appears to be a serious incompatibility between their *norms* for resolving moral dilemmas (with both norms reflecting the lower stages of moral reasoning); there is little attention given to developing a *strategy* for resolving such dilemmas (if Bill's "you shut up" is a strategy based on rules, it is developed in a thoroughly arbitrary fashion); and there is a major discrepancy in their *role-taking ability.* If this moral dilemma were to prove representative of the way that Bill and Valerie relate to each other, the pastor would have little choice but to conclude that at least one partner in this relationship lacks the capacity or will to base the marriage on a firm moral foundation. The fact that this marriage ended in divorce within a year's time provided confirming evidence for this assessment.

Moral Character Concerns

Another important facet of the moral life is the formation of moral character. A valuable resource for premarital counseling is Robert F. Peck and Robert J. Havighurst's theory of moral character.[59] This theory is based on the idea that motivation is the major determinant of character. Their own stage theory of moral development, which has certain similarities to Kohlberg's theory, is the aspect of their theory that has received the most attention. (They propose five developmental levels of character, consisting of the *amoral, expedient, conforming, irrational-conscientious,* and *rational-altruistic* stages.) But I would like to draw attention to the aspect of their theory that develops the personality correlates of moral character. Since most pastors want to gain some understanding of the personalities of the couple who come to them to be married (and sometimes use personality inventories or personal adjustment scaling devices for this purpose), the Peck and Havighurst theory has the clear merit of integrating these personality issues into a theory of moral character. Their theory centers on the following personality correlates:

1. *Perceptual System.* There are three modes of perception which are especially important for achieving a high level of moral functioning: *observation* (accurate perception of how people behave and structure their social relationships), *insight* (capacity to understand other persons' wishes, needs, and motives), and *empathy* (capacity to "feel with" another person, to experience the person's emotions and appreciate the attitudes from that person's point of view). There are obvious similarities between this and role-taking.

2. *Personality Structure.* A person's relatively permanent personality structure is an important determinant of moral behavior. Important considerations here are the maturity of

a person's *emotional reactions,* the nature of the person's most pressing *drives and impulses,* and the nature, stability, and internal congruity of the system the person has evolved to express or control emotions and impulses. Peck and Havighurst call this the *control system.*

3. *Self-Concept.* An important personality correlate of moral character is a person's concept of himself as a moral person. Is this concept accurate? That is, is he as "bad" or as "good" as he conceives himself to be? Is he able to accept responsibility for things that go wrong? What is his emotional state when he evaluates his moral behavior (calm? anxious? self-satisfied? self-critical?)? Is he able to modify his self-concept in the light of new conditions or goals?

4. *Attitudes in Major Relationships.* An important aid to understanding why a person acts morally as he does is to find out how he feels about the significant people in his life. There are two major variables in this regard. One is the *locus of concern,* representing a continuum from completely egocentric self-interest, where other people are viewed as a means to one's personal ends, to sociocentric concern, where the well-being and happiness of others is as important as one's own. The other variable is *the range of moral horizon.* How small or large is the individual's sphere of moral concern? Some people act with moral concern toward their own family members, but not toward nonfamily members (in-laws, rivals, strangers, and so forth). There are obvious parallels between this and Kohlberg's social perspective theme.

All of these personality correlates are important to the formation of moral character, but the following issues are especially germane to premarital counseling: Are the two individuals able to *empathize* with each other's feelings and attitudes? (Perceptual System.) Do they possess mature, stable, and internally congruous systems for *controlling and expressing emotions?* (Personality Structure.) Are they able to *modify their self-concept* in the light of new conditions or goals? (Self-Concept.) Are they able to appreciate the concerns of others besides themselves, including persons *outside their own immediate families?* (Attitudes in Major Relationships.) Each of these questions is important for any marriage relationship, but in some circumstances one or two will assume special importance. Ability to appreciate the concerns of in-laws is almost always important, but it takes on special importance in interfaith and interracial marriages. These four questions enable the pastor to evaluate the couple's moral maturity, and may therefore be quite useful in developing an overall assessment of their readiness for marriage. Pastors who summarize the couple's strong and weak points for the couple's benefit can use these questions to focus this summary.

Personal Virtue Concerns

A third important facet of the moral life is personal qualities, or virtue. Erik H. Erikson's approach to this issue is especially suggestive for premarital counseling. He has done much to restore virtue to a central place in developmental psychology by proposing a "schedule of virtues" to correspond to his eight stages of the life-cycle. He describes these eight virtues as inherent human qualities of strength. They are not the possession only of heroes and saints, but are basic inherent capacities which everyone possesses. They are capacities, however, that need to be reinforced by the human community. Thus, the degree to which these inherent capacities are actualized will depend to a significant extent on an individual's social experience. Columns 1 and 2 in the chart on page 142 list Erikson's life stages and human virtues. A third column indicates Donald Evans' list of eight moral virtues which also correspond to Erikson's eight stages.[60]

ERIKSON'S LIFE STAGES	ERIKSON'S HUMAN VIRTUES	EVANS' MORAL VIRTUES
Trust vs. Mistrust	Hope	Trust
Autonomy vs. Shame and Self-Doubt	Will	Humility
Initiative vs. Guilt	Purpose	Self-Acceptance
Industry vs. Inferiority	Competence	Responsibility
Identity vs. Identity Diffusion	Fidelity	Self-Commitment
Intimacy vs. Isolation	Love	Friendliness
Generativity vs. Stagnation	Care	Concern
Integrity vs. Despair	Wisdom	Contemplation

I will not attempt to discuss the relationships between Erikson's human virtues and the life stages they are associated with. This would require an extensive discussion of Erikson's life-cycle theory. Instead, I would like to draw attention to relationships between his schedule of virtues and the moral perspective of Proverbs. Proverbs makes direct or indirect reference to each one of Erikson's virtues and, as he does, identifies these as human *strengths* that are to be valued and cultivated. For Proverbs, each is an important aspect of the moral life. What follows is a small sampling of proverbs that correspond to each of Erikson's eight virtues:

Hope. "Hope deferred makes the heart sick, but a desire fulfilled is a tree of life" (13:12). "Let not your heart envy sinners, but continue in the fear of the Lord all the day.

Surely there is a future, and your hope will not be cut off" (23:17–18).

Will. "If you faint in the day of adversity, your strength is small" (24:10).

Purpose. "Prepare your work outside, get everything ready for you in the field; and after that build your house" (24:27). "Many are the plans in the mind of a man, but it is the purpose of the Lord that will be established" (19:21).

Competence. "He who is slack in his work is a brother to him who destroys" (18:9). "Do you see a man skilful in his work? he will stand before kings; he will not stand before obscure men" (22:29).

Fidelity. "Let not loyalty and faithfulness forsake you; bind them about your neck, write them on the tablet of your heart. So you will find favor and good repute in the sight of God and man" (3:3–4). "There are friends who pretend to be friends, but there is a friend who sticks closer than a brother" (18:24).

Love. "Hatred stirs up strife, but love covers all offenses" (10:12). "Better is open rebuke than hidden love" (27:5).

Care. "Train up a child in the way he should go, and when he is old he will not depart from it" (22:6).

Wisdom. "I have counsel and sound wisdom, I have insight, I have . . . strength" (8:14).

How can this correspondence between Erikson's virtues and the proverbs be used in premarital counseling? Some pastors who are sympathetic with the view that the book of Proverbs is particularly relevant to premarital counseling would like to make direct use of proverbs in their premarital counseling. But, unlike the psalms, which can be read as units, the topical diversity of the book of Proverbs makes this "unit" approach quite unworkable. An alternative approach that has been tried by some pastors is to focus on the proverbs that relate directly to the marriage relationship and the establishing of a home. This gives the Bible-reading greater coherence, but there is a clear male orientation in Proverbs' handling of the marriage relationship, and for this reason many pastors find this approach counterproductive. By organizing selected proverbs according to Erikson's schedule of virtues, the pastor is able to bring the whole moral perspective of Proverbs to bear on the couple's marriage plans, and to open discussion of the human strengths the couple will want to cultivate in their relationship together.

This use of Erikson's schedule of virtues and selected proverbs is a particularly effective way of setting the context for discussion of the wedding service itself. But, even if the pastor's schedule of virtues and corresponding selections from Proverbs are not directly introduced into the counseling process itself, they help the pastor set the appropriate tone for premarital counseling. The pastor's goal, as a representative of the supportive human community that is being asked to bless this marriage, is not to *discourage* the couple by dwelling on the problems they can be expected to encounter, but to *encourage* them toward moral growth and commitment. The pastor can do this by helping them identify and use the moral strengths that God has given them: hope, will, purpose, competence, fidelity, love, care, and wisdom. The success of their marriage will ultimately depend not on matters of chance or fate, but on their ability to use these inherent human strengths. Thus, the tone that is set in the premarital counseling session should be one that reinforces these inherent human strengths.

CONCLUSION

In taking the view that premarital counseling is *moral* education, I have undoubtedly shortchanged the *theological* concepts that are often used in premarital counseling, such as the theme of the covenant relationship, or the various proposals that have been made for understanding marriage in Christological terms. By focusing on the moral rather than theological foundations of marriage, I do not mean to suggest that theological approaches to premarital counseling are inappropriate. When theological concepts are introduced in the premarital counseling setting, however, they tend to be viewed by the couple as rather abstract ideas that do not relate very well to the issues at hand. Yes, they want to view their marriage as a "covenantal relationship," and yes, they see themselves as entering marriage "in the name of Christ." But, for the most part, they find these concepts difficult to relate, except in a very general way, to their current anxieties, apprehensions, hopes, and aspirations. Premarital counseling that emphasizes the moral foundation of marriage, especially when this involves exploration of specific moral experiences and commitments, is able to address these concerns in a more concrete and helpful way. In my judgment, premarital counseling is "the proper time" to focus on the *moral* foundations of marriage.

One final matter. Given my proposal for the use of Kohlberg's stage theory of moral reasoning in premarital counseling, it is only natural to ask whether Proverbs itself reflects a certain stage of moral reasoning? If so, does this invalidate the whole idea of using the moral perspective of Proverbs in premarital counseling? In my judgment, it *is* the case that Proverbs reflects a certain level of moral reasoning, that it is somewhere between stage 3 (conformity to social expectation) and stage 4 (support of social laws and civic responsibility) in its moral orientation. But this does not invalidate it as a basis for premarital counseling, because precisely these moral stages provide the essential ingredients of a morally mature marriage relationship. In their social perspectives, stage 3 emphasizes "stable, continuing, and meaningful relationships based on affection" and stage 4 supports "development of an ordering structure for interpersonal relationships."[61] These are basic to the moral foundations of marriage. Thus, on the basis of moral developmental theory itself, the moral perspective of Proverbs is appropriate for premarital counseling. Married persons may, of course, achieve higher stages of moral development, both inside and outside the marriage relationship. But the basic moral foundations of marriage are supplied by stage 3 and stage 4 morality.

Unfortunately, many marriages today are based on the morality of the *earlier* stages. In many cases, the marriage relationship "is composed of little powerless persons and big authorities who are in control" (stage 1) or is "based on useful exchange" with very limited ability to put oneself in the other's position (stage 2). Thus, the goal of premarital counseling is not to establish the marriage relationship on a stage 5 or stage 6 moral foundation, but to ensure that the marriage will not be based on stage 1 or stage 2 morality. Unlike the moral perspective of Proverbs, these lower stages reinforce the "myth" that marriage is inevitably a losing proposition for one, if not both, participants in the marriage relationship.

Chapter 4

The Use of Parables
and Marriage Counseling

Jesus' parables have often puzzled readers of the Bible. While concerned with everyday events, they nevertheless convey unexpected religious insights. In contrast to proverbs, parables in their content as narratives deal with change and transformation, often with unpredictable results. The need to interpret the parables has similarities to the process of counseling, which involves the narrative and reinterpretation of the counselee's own life story. Such reinterpretation is particularly valuable for people seeking help for troubled marriages.

In this chapter we will first take up the common view in pastoral counseling literature that the parable is essentially a moral lesson. Then we will consider the more promising view that parables concern perceptual change. Next we will look at views of recent biblical scholars about the nature of parables, centering on the narrative form, metaphorical structure, and types of parables. On the basis of these views I will then develop an approach to pastoral counseling focused on perceptual reorganization. This discussion will draw on Gestalt theory and Carl Rogers' view of counseling. The chapter will conclude with treatment specifically of marriage counseling, suggesting ways in which the parables may be useful in clarifying and interpreting the relationship of husband and wife.

The parables of Jesus provide us with a third approach to the Bible's role in pastoral counseling, one that is uniquely different from the two that we have already discussed. In terms of counseling method, this approach is neither non-directive nor directive, but *in* directive. In its understanding of the process of personal change, its focus is not the exploration of *feelings* or *moral behavior,* but the reorganization of *perceptions.* Because its method and objectives are significantly different from the other two approaches, this approach challenges the simplistic but commonly held view that pastoral counseling methods are to be understood in terms of a polarity between directive and nondirective counseling. This is fitting, because a major function of Jesus' parables was to take existing social and cultural polarities (Jews vs. Samaritans, Pharisees vs. publicans, masters vs. servants) and to challenge the perceptions that had created them.

PREVIOUS INTERPRETATIONS OF PARABLES AND COUNSELING

Unlike the two previous approaches to the Bible's role in pastoral counseling, the parabolic approach has no strong advocates. There are very few references to the parables in literature on the use of the Bible in counseling, and even these references reflect a view of the parables that is now obsolete. Carroll Wise probably gives more direct attention to the parables than any other writer. But he views the parables as moral teachings, a view that is no longer considered valid by biblical scholars.[62]

For example, he contends that the parable of the Good Samaritan provides a model of service to one's neighbor. Unlike the priest and the Levite, the Samaritan "was free to feel with the suffering man, and feeling with him, having compassion, was moved to do what obviously needed to be done." Wise says that, in contrast, the third servant in the parable of the Talents was unable to provide effective service because he was immobilized by fear. It was fear that caused him to bury the talents he had been given, and to rationalize his inaction ("Master, I knew you to be a hard man"). Thus, the good Samaritan was able to serve effectively because he was motivated by love, while the third servant failed to serve because he was overcome with fear. These two parables, therefore, serve as moral examples. The good Samaritan's behavior is extolled because it reflects positive motives, while the third servant's behavior is condemned because it reflects negative motives.

Wise's interpretations of the parables of the Prodigal Son and the Ten Bridesmaids also emphasize their value as moral examples. These two parables illustrate crises that arise in life "because something is wrong in the way we are living, in our real feelings and relationships." The prodigal son experienced God's judgment as he sat among the swine. He then "judged himself in the light of a more ideal situation, and took the necessary steps to move toward that situation." In contrast, the ten bridesmaids refused "to meet the necessary conditions which are imposed by the nature of life." They learned the hard way that we are not "permitted to enter into any satisfying experience until we have met conditions necessary for that experience," including learning to live by our own insights and not depending exclusively on the guidance of others. Thus, these two parables teach us that individuals experience crises in their lives because they have been unwilling or unable to live up to life's responsibilities. The Prodigal Son story indicates, however, that if one makes the effort to gain insight into the reasons for failure to meet life's responsibilities, one's situation can be turned around.

Wise discusses other parables, but these are sufficient to illustrate his view that the parables are moral teachings. The uniqueness of his understanding of the parables as moral examples is that he focuses on the inner feelings of individuals who are confronted with the challenge to act responsibly. What enables a person to act responsibly is the formation of positive feelings and attitudes (such as love), and what inhibits a person from acting responsibly is being controlled by negative feelings and attitudes (such as fear and self-indulgence). Thus, if one's actions are irresponsible, one needs to achieve insight into one's underlying feelings and motives to determine the source of this impediment to positive moral action.

Wayne Oates's brief comments on the parables reflect a similar concern with their value as moral teachings.[63] He contends that the parable "is the most used means of instruction whereby the Bible may be applied redemptively to the problems people present a pastor in a counseling session." Then, to illustrate the parable's instructional uses, he cites Jesus' parable of the Rich Fool. In Luke's account, this parable is preceded by a request from a man in the crowd, "Teacher, bid my brother divide the inheritance with me." Jesus responded, "Man, who made me a judge or divider over you?" and then proceeded to tell the story of the Rich Fool as a warning against "all covetousness." Oates contends that Jesus was faced here with one of the "thorniest of family counseling problems" (the division of a family fortune), but he refused to be placed in the role of a judge. Rather, he "redefined himself as a teacher by telling the unforgettable parable of the Rich Fool and his barns." Then, to reinforce what he had taught through the parable, he added the proverbial saying: "So is he who lays up treasure for himself, and is not rich toward God."

Oates believes that this parable is concerned with a difficult moral dilemma, that is, the rightful division of the family inheritance. Jesus refuses to play the judge, but he does not hesitate to assume the role of the moral teacher. He warns about covetousness, tells a story that illustrates its grave moral dangers, and then relates a proverb that teaches one to find treasure not in oneself but in God. Thus, Jesus wanted the man who asked the question to make a good moral decision, so he told a story that probed the covetous feelings and attitudes that lay behind the question. In identifying and probing these attitudes, Jesus succeeded admirably as a moral teacher. He did not deal with the question on the surface level, as a judge might have done, but instead probed the attitude behind the question, as a good moral teacher would do. Thus, Oates could say with Wise that this parable challenges readers to make "a deep examination and modification of their feelings and attitudes," and shows that Jesus himself has deep "insight into the dynamics of human personality."

While Wise and Oates view the parables as moral lessons, James E. Dittes offers a different view of parables, one that is consistent with the approach that I will be developing in this chapter. In his various writings, he makes considerable use of what we might call "living parables"—the Bible study class that persists in resisting the assigned topic; a deacon who has great difficulty in following the Communion distribution procedure; a junior high Sunday school class that practices the biblical injunction to "turn the other cheek"; a minister and board of elders who explore their attitudes about home visitation.[64]

Dittes occasionally alludes to Jesus' own parables when developing these stories. In *The Church in the Way,* he discusses the case of a church school teacher who had been disheartened when two boys disrupted a carefully planned dramatization of the Prodigal Son story by breaking from the group and wrestling in the corner. As she reflected on this "disciplinary problem," she "suddenly discovered—with an audible 'aha'—that she had a real-life 'play within a play' right there in her room." In *The Minister on the Spot,* Dittes' comparison of preaching to four ways of going out on a limb (guaranteed soft landing, clinging to the guaranteed limb, freedom as obligation, and assurance is in the breaking) is reminiscent of Jesus' parable of the Sower. But it is in his more recent book, *When the People Say No,* that Dittes begins to develop the approach to parables that I will be advocating here. In this book, he does not allude to Jesus' own parables, but he treats Acts' narrative of Peter and John's encounter with the beggar at the Beautiful Gate as though it can be interpreted as a parable of healing. He suggests that this story is an instance of how we can "see through" our normal expectations to find healing and transformative change. The account says that Peter fixed his eyes on the man and that, in turn, the man was all attention because he expected a gift from Peter and John. Dittes asks: "When Peter looked at the man, what did he see? He saw a beggar, yes. He also saw a cripple. He also saw a whole man. To fix his eyes on *him,* to see him wholly, to minister to him, Peter needed to see all three." In seeing the man whole, Peter saw through the man's own expectations and turned the episode from mere almsgiving to an act of healing. It was his ability to see through the man's normal expectations that set the stage for the healing that followed.[65]

Since the story of Peter and John's encounter with the beggar at the Beautiful Gate can be interpreted as a "parable," Dittes' interpretation of this story invites a different view of Jesus' parables from the views of Wise and Oates. Dittes' interpretation suggests that, instead of viewing the parable in moral terms, as though it were intended to teach a moral lesson, we should view it in perceptual terms as a story intended to challenge our normal perceptions of things. In this view, the change that the parable achieves is not more responsible behavior but a transformed outlook on life.

Significantly, this view of the parable is receiving increasing support among biblical scholars. Most biblical scholars now recognize that the parables are not intended to provide moral instruction but to alter our normal perceptions, especially of God's activity in the world. Like the story of the beggar who experiences the healing power of God in a totally unexpected way, the parables open the listener to a wholly new perception of how God acts in life. Since moral lessons typically reinforce the perceptions we already hold of God and his expectations of us, the parables are radically different from moral lessons.

According to biblical scholars, a major reason that Jesus' parables have been misread as moral instruction is that, very early in the development of the Christian community, they were being reinterpreted in terms of normal moral expectations. Luke's account of the parable of the Rich Fool, which Oates interpreted as an example of Jesus' moral instruction, is a case in point. Here, the Gospel writer has placed the original parable within a moral framework. The Lukan account begins with a man raising a moral issue and closes with a proverb that makes a moral point about covetousness. However, if the parable is removed from the moral framework that Luke provides, it is not a story about a covetous man, but of a man who *misperceived* his true situation. In the original version, the issue is not that the "rich fool" was "rich," consumed by greed, but that he was a "fool" for planning for the future when his death was imminent. As John Dominic Crossan points out, the original parable was undoubtedly "a simple story of tragic irony in which a man spends his last day on earth planning a long future. A very definite but utterly human example of failure to realize one's true situation."[66] Thus, when the parables are removed from the moral framework in which they were subsequently placed, they appear not as moral lessons, but as stories in which normal perceptions of our situation are challenged and overturned.

Since this alternative view of the parables is fundamental to the parabolic approach to pastoral counseling, we need to take an in-depth look at biblical scholars' views, centering on the parable's *narrative form* and its *metaphorical structure.*

RECENT SCHOLARS' VIEWS OF THE NATURE OF PARABLES

The Narrative Form

Jesus' parables are stories. They take a narrative form. And since the content of the Bible is inseparable from the forms through which it communicates, we need to take seriously the fact that Jesus' message was communicated in story form. What kind of stories are they? What are the formal characteristics of this particular story form, and how do these characteristics serve the intentions of the storyteller?

Sallie McFague TeSelle integrates much recent biblical scholarship on precisely these questions in her book *Speaking in Parables.*[67] What kind of stories are the parables? She points out that they are fundamentally stories about *individuals* in the process of *coming to belief:* "It is not intellectual belief or momentary experience that is revealed in these stories, but the style of life or belief chosen through a myriad of decisions and now come to a head." The individuals whose processes of "coming to belief" are captured in these stories are caught in *characteristic action* "at the moment in their lives when they are most themselves, when they reveal themselves most precisely and definitively." Thus, the parables are stories about individuals. But this does not mean that they reflect an individualistic perspective. On the contrary, "The sort of action we find in the parables . . . is always decisions in regard to other people—fathers and sons, masters and servants, husbands and wives, citizens and rulers." The world which these stories project is a public not privatistic world, with an individual's coming to belief portrayed not as an inner experience but as a decision involving relationships with other persons.

If the world that these stories project is a public not privatistic world, it is also a remarkably secular world. The parables do not actually talk about God or spiritual matters, and the human actions they describe are not characteristically "religious" acts. Rather, the actions they tell about involve home, commerce, agriculture, travel, and so forth. They are peculiarly "nonreligious." On the other hand, the stories are *indirectly* about the kingdom or activity of God: "The parabolic story may be . . . the indirect genre par excellence." The parable tells about individuals making decisions at critical junctures in their lives, but the listener senses that the story is about "something more" than a wage dispute, a wedding party, or even an act of compassion, and this something more is the activity of God in the world. The parable is indirectly about God. The critical decisions reached by the individuals in these stories are self-revealing, but they are also revealing of the way God acts in human lives.

TeSelle uses the term "metaphor" to get at the parable's indirection, and calls the parable an "extended metaphor." The metaphorical structure of the parable is its most important formal characteristic, and it serves Jesus' intentions by enabling him to speak indirectly of the activity of God. What makes metaphor a vehicle of indirection is the fact that, with metaphors, "we use the conventional wisdom associated with one context to serve as the screen or grid through which we see the other context." Normally, the context that serves as the screen or grid is one we know something about, while the other context is one we know little about but want to know more. Thus, the Gospel of John uses the metaphor of a mansion with rooms to describe the place which Jesus is preparing for his followers. Similarly, Jesus' parables are metaphoric because they use contexts of ordinary human action to provide insight into the realm of God's extraordinary action.

In short, the narrative form of the parable portrays individuals in interaction with other persons, and through this interaction they are being propelled toward a crisis calling for decisive action. This narrative form of interaction⟶ crisis ⟶ decision is itself a metaphor for what things are like in God's sphere of activity. In that context, it is appropriate to call this pattern of interaction⟶ crisis⟶ decision a process of coming to belief. This is clearly not an intellectual belief, but a convictional experience of God's acting in human life. To explore the parables' understanding of this experience, we need to take a more detailed look at the metaphorical structure of Jesus' parables. For this I will focus on the writings of John Dominic Crossan.

The Metaphorical Structure

The book of Proverbs makes much use of metaphorical figures of speech. This simile is typical: "A man without self-control is like a city broken into and left without walls" (Prov. 25:28). Such figures are what C. S. Lewis calls metaphors "which we invent to teach by."[68] The author wants to make a pedagogical point, and the chosen metaphor is one among many possible figures that could have been chosen to make the same didactic point. The metaphors in Jesus' parables are quite different. As Crossan points out, Jesus' metaphors "articulate a referent so new or so alien to consciousness that this referent can only be grasped within the metaphor itself." Thus the metaphor does not make a point, it embodies a reality.

The reality which Jesus' metaphors embody is the kingdom of God, understood not as a place or a region, or even as a reign or a kingship, but as divine activity. As Paul Ricoeur points out, the kingdom of God "is not compared to

the man who . . . to the woman who . . . to the yeast which
. . . but to *what happens* in the story."[69] Thus, the parable is
ultimately not about a divine place, or a divine state of affairs,
but divine activity. Furthermore, the parable does not merely
teach *about* this activity, it draws the listener into the very
experience of it. As Crossan puts it, the metaphor's "power
creates the participation whereby its truth is experienced."
Thus, in contrast to the metaphor that the *teacher* chooses
in order to make a didactic point, it is the *metaphor* that does
the choosing as it draws the listener into immediate participation in the reality to which it refers: "There are metaphors
in which information precedes participation so that the function of metaphor is to illustrate information about the metaphor's referent; but there are also metaphors in which participation precedes information so that the function of metaphor
is to create participation in the metaphor's referent." Thus,
the parable is essentially not a teaching method, using metaphorical language to inform one's listeners about the kingdom of God. Instead, it is an *event* in which listeners participate in God's activity.

But what is the nature of this event? What form of participation is involved? To Crossan, it is essentially a perceptual
event. Through the metaphorical structure of the parable,
one is enabled to participate in God's activity through a new
perceptual experience. The experience of God's activity is
inseparable from one's perception of it because the "moment
of perception" *is* that experience. Thus, Crossan contends
that Jesus' intention is to induce listeners to experience God's
activity in their very perception of it.

The parables are not concerned with any and every conceivable experience of God. As Ricoeur points out, "The first
thing that may strike us is that the Parables are radically
profane stories—there are no gods, no demons, no angels, no
miracles, no time before time, as in the creation stories, not
even founding events as in the Exodus account." Instead,

they tell about "ordinary people doing ordinary things: selling and buying, letting down a net into the seas, and so on. Here resides the initial paradox: on the one hand, these stories are . . . narratives of normalcy—but on the other hand, it is the Kingdom of God that is said to be like this. The paradox is that the *extraordinary is like the ordinary.*"

Thus, if Jesus' metaphors are alien to the normal consciousness of his listeners, this is not because they are foreign or esoteric, but because they allude to phenomena and activities that are so well known as to be almost routine, of merely passing interest. On the other hand, his metaphors challenge this view of common events as merely routine and mundane by using such events to communicate his experience of God. As Crossan points out, the fact that Jesus used such materials in developing his metaphors is one reason that the church, as early as the Gospels, has found it relatively easy to reduce the radicality of his vision to normal expectations of how God acts. Such reductions have had the unfortunate effect of muting, if not entirely eliminating, the paradox that is at the core of Jesus' experience of God—that the extraordinary is like the ordinary.

Types of Parables

Jesus' paradoxical use of metaphors raises a question that opens up discussion of the parables themselves: What was it about his metaphors that made them so alien to his listeners' normal perceptions of how God acts? One can see why his use of routine and mundane events for his metaphors might be offensive to listeners who expected more lofty allusions. But this, of itself, would not challenge their normal perception of things. What enabled his metaphors to challenge, even undermine, these normal perceptions of how God acts? This question takes us to Crossan's analysis of individual parables, which he categorizes into three types, reflecting the three modalities of the activity of God. These are parables in which *advent, reversal,* or *action* predominate. In all three types, the metaphorical structure of the parable breaks through normal expectations of God and creates a whole new perception of how he acts in human lives.

A good parable to start with is the Treasure because, as Crossan points out, it includes all three modalities. It is a very brief parable: "The kingdom of heaven is like a treasure hidden in a field, which a man found and covered up; then in his joy he goes and sells all that he has and buys that field" (Matt. 13:44). With this parable, we confront a man whose normal perceptions of past, present, and future are rudely but happily shattered: "The future he had presumably planned and projected for himself is totally invalidated by the *advent* of the Treasure which opens up a new world and unforeseen possibilities. In the face of this advent he willingly *reverses* his entire past, quite rightly and wisely he sells 'all that he has.' And from this advent and reversal he obtains the Treasure which now distorts his time and his history in the most literal and concrete sense of these words. It gives him a new world of life and *action* he did not have before and he could not have programmed for himself." Thus, all three modalities of the kingdom of God—advent, reversal, action—are present in this brief parable about the hidden treasure. When the man experienced the "advent" of the treasure, the other two modalities also broke in upon him, as his whole world underwent a total reversal and he began to act out of a totally new perception of his situation in the world. Jesus challenges his listeners to enter into this man's experience, of the happy shattering of his world. In doing so, they will experience God's ability to appear without prior warning, to turn one's world upside down, and to set a whole new agenda for one's life. With this paradigmatic parable as background, let's now turn to parables that reflect one or another of these three modalities. We begin with the parable of advent.

Advent Parables

Crossan classifies parables in which advent is the primary modality according to three types. There are parables in which the advent of the kingdom reflects *hiddenness and mystery,* such as the Fig Tree (Mark 13:28; Matt. 24:32; Luke 21:29–30) and the Leaven (Matt. 13:33; Luke 13:20–21). Others emphasize *gift and surprise,* such as the Sower (Mark 4:3–8; Matt. 13:3–8; Luke 8:5–8) and the Mustard Seed (Mark 4:30–32; Matt. 13:31–32; Luke 13:18–19). In a third group, *discovery and joy* predominate, such as the Lost Sheep (Matt. 18:12–13; Luke 15:4–6) and the Lost Coin (Luke 15:8–9).

Crossan offers a detailed analysis of the two gift and surprise parables in his book *In Parables.* He has briefer analyses of the discovery and joy parables in *The Dark Interval.* I will confine my comments to the two parables of gift and surprise —the Sower and the Mustard Seed. I will not try to reconstruct his exegetical analyses of these parables, but will focus only on his conclusions.

In both cases, Crossan concludes that, contrary to common belief, Jesus' metaphors do not depict God's activity as steady increments of growth. Rather, in both parables, there are sharp juxtapositions of two states of affairs. In the Sower, three instances of sowing losses and three instances of sowing gains are in sharp contrast. An equally dramatic contrast is evident in the Mustard Seed, with the small seed juxtaposed to the large shade of the plant. Crossan acknowledges that, in both parables, "there is growth present and of course the biblical mind was aware of such growth." But, given these sharp juxtapositions, the parables do not emphasize "growth but miracle, not organic and biological development, but the gift-like nature, the graciousness and the surprise of the ordinary, the advent of bountiful harvest despite the losses of sowing, the large shade despite the small seed."

Thus, Jesus uses metaphors of natural growth and development. But instead of using conventional observations of how natural phenomena grow and develop, Jesus undermines them, and portrays the growth in ways that conventional wisdom would consider fanciful and absurd. Thus, he offers an unorthodox view of the natural world and likens the activity of God to this new and strange perception of how things grow. The bountiful harvest is not the culmination of successful sowings, but occurs precisely where there have been severe sowing losses. Thus, it is a "distorted" view of the natural world that is used to shed light on God's sphere of activity.

The parable of the Mustard Seed also develops a metaphor for the kingdom of God drawn from the natural world. As in the Sower parable, Jesus portrays growth as a miracle, not as an incremental process. In a twinkling of an eye, the lowly mustard seed is a huge shrub. This challenge to conventional wisdom about how growth occurs overturns traditional understandings of the kingdom of God. As Crossan points out, Jesus intends his Mustard Seed parable to challenge the traditional apocalyptic image of the mighty cedar of Lebanon. While the Synoptic Gospels attempt to integrate the parable into this apocalyptic tradition, Crossan argues that Jesus intended his parable to subvert traditional apocalyptic expectations generated by this image of the mighty cedar of Lebanon. In fact, Crossan inclines to the view that his intention was to lampoon this tradition, especially the pretentiousness implicit in its choice of imagery. Thus, both advent parables challenge our normal perceptions of how things work, and through this challenge, induce listeners to experience God's activity in a whole new way. To those who believe that God's sphere of activity grows in steady increments, these two parables portray God's creative activity as an unanticipated breakthrough, as gift and surprise.

Reversal Parables

Parables in which reversal predominates include the Good Samaritan (Luke 10:30–37), the Rich Man and Lazarus (Luke 16:19–31), the Pharisee and the Publican (Luke 18:10–14), the Wedding Guest (Luke 14:1–24), the Proper Guests (Luke 14:12–14), the Great Supper (Matt. 22:1–10; Luke 14:16–24), and the Prodigal Son (Luke 15:11–32). As Crossan observes, Luke views many of these parables as example stories, providing models of good and/or bad ethical action. The "metaphorical point" of these parables, however, was not to offer a moral lesson, but to portray the kingdom of God breaking abruptly into human consciousness and demanding the overturn of prior values, closed options, set judgments, and established convictions. Crossan calls this overturn a complete or "polar" reversal. If *either* the last becomes first *or* the first becomes last, we have a single reversal. But if the last becomes first *and* the first becomes last, we have a polar reversal. The effect of this more radical reversal is to undermine confidence in the world we have constructed for ourselves: "When the north pole becomes the south pole, and the south the north, a world is reversed and overturned and we find ourselves standing firmly on utter uncertainty. The parables of reversal intend to do precisely this to our security because such is the advent of the Kingdom."

The Good Samaritan story is an excellent example of such polar reversal. As we have already seen, this parable is often viewed as an example story, evoking commendations of the Samaritan for either his neighborliness or his response to the law of love. But Crossan contends that the significance of the story is in its polar reversal. The story represents the despised Samaritan as a "good" man, whereas the respected priest and Levite are portrayed as "bad" men. Hence, a polar reversal has taken place. If Jesus had simply wanted to teach the importance of love of one's neighbor, he could have used the standard threesome, as he does in his stories involving servants, with one person's actions commended as an expression of love, another's viewed as above reproach, and a third's judged unacceptable. If he had wanted to teach neighborliness, and at the same time take a satirical poke at the clerical circles of Jerusalem, he could have used a priest, a Levite, and a Jewish layperson. If he had wanted to teach neighborliness to enemies as well as to friends, he could have had a Jew assist a Samaritan. By making the Samaritan "good," the parable is not meant to serve as a moral example, but instead "demands that one say what cannot be said, what is a contradiction in terms: Good + Samaritan."

Crossan does not deny that this parable describes a moral action, and that it takes absolutely for granted that assisting the man in need was required in such a case. Otherwise, the failure of the priest and Levite to act would not have been so disgraceful. But he points out that the parable has a literal and a metaphorical level, with the moral action of the story making the literal but not the metaphorical point of the parable: "There is a literal point which stems from the surface level of the story, and a metaphorical one which lives on a much deeper level and appears in a mysterious dialectic with the former point. In distinction to this, of course, [the] example [story] has only one, literal level."

With parables involving the world of nature, listeners are not likely to mistake the literal point for the metaphorical point. One "knows" that the story is not only about farming or small shrubs. But in parables that deal with moral actions, especially positive moral acts, there is a great danger of confusing the two levels of the story: "If the protagonist is presented in a downright immoral action, confusion ensues, but at least the distinction between literal and metaphorical is usually maintained." In a parable like the Good Samaritan, where the protagonist performs a morally good action on the literal level, "It is very simple to remain on this level and convert the parable into example." When this happens, the metaphorical level, with its reversal of normal expectations, is overlooked.

On the other hand, the literal and metaphorical levels are not totally separate. They would appear to be so if the literal meaning of the Good Samaritan parable were simply that good moral actions are to be commended. But, in fact, the literal level is more complex than that. On the literal level, Jesus expressed the unspeakable thought that a Samaritan might be "good" and the Jewish religious leaders simultaneously "bad." Thus, "the literal point confronted the hearers with the necessity of saying the impossible and having their world turned upside down and radically questioned in its presuppositions." This confrontation on the literal level introduced them to the metaphorical point of the parable, that in the very same way the kingdom of God turns our world upside down and radically questions its presuppositions. Hence, "the hearer struggling with the contradictory dualism of Good/Samaritan is actually experiencing in and through this the inbreaking of the Kingdom. Not only does it happen like this, it happens in this."

In briefer analyses of the other parables of reversal, Crossan shows that, in each case, the metaphorical structure of the parable is based on polar reversal. His comments on the Pharisee and the Publican parable illustrate the radical nature of this reversal, because in this story there is a reversal of accepted *religious* as well as *moral* judgments. Jesus challenges his listeners to imagine a situation in which the virtuous Pharisee is rejected by God and the sinful publican gains God's approval. If they can imagine this, they have begun to perceive and experience the kingdom of God. As Crossan puts it, the metaphorical challenge is clear: What if God does not play the game by our rules?

Given our previous discussion of Proverbs, Crossan's contention that Jesus' *proverbs* employ the technique of polar reversal is especially noteworthy. Jesus' use of proverbs ("It is easier for a camel to go through the eye of a needle than for a rich man to enter the kingdom of God") has led some commentators to suggest that this places him within the tradition of Israel's wisdom literature. But Crossan contends that this apparent link to ancient wisdom literature is largely due to the Gospel writers' concern to tone down the mysterious radicality of Jesus' proverbs. For example, the radical polar reversal in the proverb, "For to him who has will more be given; and from him who has not will be taken away" has been altered to read, "and from him who has not, even what he thinks that he has will be taken away" (Luke 8:18). In other words, the notion that a person can lose "nothing" does not make sense to Luke, so he modifies the proverb to explain how "nothing" really means "the appearance of something." Such modification brings Jesus' proverbs into line with Proverbs' strategy of basing its convictions on the observable world, the world of normal expectations, but they distort the original intentions behind his proverbs.

Jesus' unorthodox use of the proverb form alerts us to fundamental differences between his reversal parables and Proverbs. Proverbs encourages confidence in the stable *moral* order of life. But Jesus' parables undermine this confidence by asserting that paradox is a fundamental reality in the kingdom of God. In the kingdom, one who has nothing can lose what one does not have. There is no such "mysterious radicality" in the moral world view of Proverbs. The authors of Proverbs recognize that human experience has its puzzling features, even its contradictions, but they do not accord any ultimate value to the radical paradox implicit in polar reversal. Thus, Jesus challenges the world view of Proverbs when he says that, as the last become first, the first become last. And when Crossan argues that parables of reversal are not example stories designed to inspire moral action, he is contending that the "world" these parables overturn is the world that Proverbs takes for granted. His argument in *The Dark Interval* that *parable* is the binary opposite of *myth* reinforces this contention. If the "myth" of Proverbs establishes a "world" in which confidence in the moral order of things is justified, Jesus' parables subvert this myth by challenging its assumption that the ultimate order of life (that is, the activity of God) can be readily extrapolated from our own moral order. What if God does not play the game by our rules?

Action Parables

In discussing parables of action, Crossan continues to challenge the view that parables are moral examples that tell us what we ought to do. The protagonists in many of these parables engaged in actions that were either moral or immoral, and thus open to ethical assessment. But the purpose of these action parables is not to teach moral lessons. If anything, they intend for us "to experience how the logic of ethics is undermined by the mystery of God and *that,* if one can but accept it, is the most crucial moral experience of all."

Action parables that give unmistakable clues to the fact that Jesus' stories are not moral examples are the Friend at Midnight (Luke 11:5–8) and the Judge and the Importunate Widow (Luke 18:2–5). In both cases, the protagonist does not pretend to act from considered moral conviction, but simply accepts the bothersome inevitability of what must be done. If these parables were moral examples, their moral counsel would be something like: Respond to neighbors and adversaries' entreaties so that they will quit bothering you. When they are reduced to this form, we can see immediately that these parables are not intended to inspire moral action. In fact, the judge in the second parable says explicitly that his action is not based on any sense of morality. In Crossan's view, what these parables do, therefore, is to draw attention to the *moment of decision.* Whether this moment comes suddenly, in the middle of the night, or whether it comes after one has delayed as long as possible, it inevitably comes. Thus, these parables of action "portray crucial or critical situations which demand firm and resolute action, prompt and energetic decision."

The critical moment calling for decisive action is reflected in all parables of action, which include the Way to Judgment (Luke 12:58–59; Matt. 5:25–26), the Fig Tree (Luke 13:6–9), the Seed Growing Secretly (Mark 4:26–29), the Thief in the Night (Matt. 24:43–44; Luke 12:39–40), the Tower Builder and the Campaign Planner (Luke 14:28–32), the Rich Fool (Luke 12:16–20), the Wedding Garment (Matt. 22:11–14), the Ten Bridesmaids (Matt. 25:1–13), and the servant parables, which Crossan divides into two groups. The first group of servant parables includes the Doorkeeper (Mark 13:33–37; Luke 12:35–38), the Overseer (Matt. 24:45–51; Luke 12: 42–46), the Talents (Matt. 25:14–30; Luke 19:12–27), and the Throne Claimant (Luke 19:12b, 14–15a, 27). The second group of servant parables includes the Unmerciful Servant (Matt. 18:23–35), the Servant's Reward (Luke 17:7–10), the Unjust Steward (Luke 16:1–9), the Wicked Husbandmen (Mark 12:1–12; Matt. 21:33–46; Luke 20:9–19), and the Vineyard Workers (Matt. 20:1–16).

In his detailed discussion of the servant parables, Crossan notes that all involve a master-servant relationship at the moment of *critical reckoning.* In the first group of servant parables, the resolution of this moment of critical reckoning has a certain normalcy about it. At the critical moment, "Good or faithful or successful servants are rewarded; bad and faithless and unsuccessful servants are punished." But the second group reverses this normal pattern, functioning as the polar reversal of the first group. In these parables, "this horizon of expected normalcy is not so apparent and . . . is questioned, probed, and finally contradicted." Good servants are not rewarded, and bad servants are not punished. The parable of the Vineyard Workers is the most complete reversal of this expected normalcy, for the good workers do not get what they expect and the other workers get more than they deserve. Hence, in the servant parables, Jesus told stories that supported the expectations of the normal moral order of things, but he also told stories that undermined these expectations. The crucial metaphorical point of the servant parables, taken as a whole, is not that some actions are good and others are bad, but that, in the kingdom of God, we cannot place confidence in our normal expectations of what will be judged good or bad.

In effect, therefore, these action parables make the same metaphorical point as reversal parables. Confidence in the moral order of life is unwarranted when considered in the light of God's activity. If some parables seem to support this confidence, others negate it. Those which negate it are especially crucial because their presence in the corpus is itself enough to challenge such confidence and to induce us to participate in the mystery of God: "They remove our defences and make us vulnerable to God. It is only in such experiences that God can touch us, and only in such moments does the kingdom of God arrive." Crossan calls such vulnerability the experience of transcendence, and adds: "Perhaps it is only in moments of mortal jeopardy that this exclusion of security comes most deeply home to consciousness. At such times we best realize that security is the serenity that comes from accepting insecurity as our mortal lot."

But, if action parables make the same metaphorical point as reversal parables, their emphasis on the moment of critical reckoning is unique. When a servant is called to account by his master, the issue is not whether the servant was previously good or bad, but how he meets this new crisis of reckoning. The good servant cannot rely on the fact that he has been good in the past, nor can the bad servant avoid the crisis on the grounds that his fate is already decided, for he is confronted with the warning that "from him who has not will be taken away." Thus, both face a crisis of reckoning whose outcome cannot be predicted on the basis of normal expectation. In the Vineyard Workers parable, those who worked all day expected to be paid more than those who did not, and those who came late undoubtedly expected to be paid less. But neither expectation was supported. The metaphorical point of this parable is not that the vineyard owner was an unusually generous man (as Matthew suggests), but that he is one who violates expectations. That the servants' expectations can be absolutely reversed by the master introduces an awesome uncertainty into the master-servant relationship, and makes the crisis of reckoning a frightening event.

On the other hand, Crossan stresses that the servant faced with his crisis of reckoning is not a helpless pawn. In a number of servant parables, the master challenges the servant to be resourceful and decisive. The unjust steward, for example, is hardly a paragon of virtue. His response to his crisis of reckoning could not possibly be held up as a moral example, but he was able to act resourcefully in his crisis of reckoning and his master commended him for it. Jesus implies here that the advent of the kingdom of God calls for similar resourceful and resolute actions, actions made difficult by the fact that one has no secure moral or religious grounds on which to base them.

Moreover, as the Ten Bridesmaids, also an action parable, indicates, some will not act until it is too late. Paul Ricoeur points out that this parable, one of those which Joachim Jeremias termed the "It May Be Too Late" parables, runs "counter to actual experience where there will always be another chance. . . . At what village wedding has anyone slammed the door on the frivolous maidens who do not consider the future (and who are, after all, as carefree as the lilies of the field)?" In violating actual experience, this parable is as foreign to reality in the sphere of human interaction as the Sower and the Mustard Seed are to the realities of the natural world. But this "foreignness" enables Jesus to make the metaphorical point that the kingdom of God subverts the normal expectation that there will always be time to act. In effect, what is subverted here is the expectation created by Proverbs' "doctrine of the proper time," the conviction that we can know the proper time to act. The parables that fall into the "It May Be Too Late" category (Matt. 24:36 to 25:13) challenge our confidence that we will know the proper time to act. Indeed, Jesus invites his listeners to consider the possibility, and thus imagine the unimaginable, that in regard to the kingdom of God, the "proper time" for them to act has already passed.

Crossan's interpretations of advent, reversal, and action parables could be discussed in much greater detail. But this summary makes the point which is central to our interests here, that the experience underlying Jesus' parables is the radical restructuring of normal perceptions of God's activity in the world. Through the parables, one sees God's activity in a wholly new light. And this "seeing" or "perceiving" is itself a participation in God's activity. As we begin to explore the implications of Jesus' parables for pastoral counseling, we will be focusing our attention on his use of this narrative form to challenge our normal perceptions of how God acts in our lives, and to induce us to enter into a perceptual world in which it is God who breaks the rules.

ALTERNATIVE APPROACH TO THE USE OF PARABLES IN COUNSELING

A. Change Through Perceptual Experience

As we have seen, the changes that the parables effect in their listeners are perceptual ones. Participation in Jesus' parables leads to a totally new experience of God's activity, which in turn effects a radical change in our perception of our situation. Normal perceptions of our world are reversed. The north pole becomes the south pole, and the south the north.

The parables' emphasis on change through perceptual experience has important implications for pastoral marriage counseling. If properly understood, it can shape the methods, objectives, and counselor-counselee relationship in pastoral counseling. To achieve this understanding, I will explore the parables' emphasis on change through perceptual experience with the perceptual categories of classical Gestalt psychology. The three major categories of Gestalt theory of perception that are especially relevant here are perceptual reorganization, figure-ground relationships, and pattern completion (or what gestaltists call the "law of good continuation"). In discussing each of these issues, I am concerned not to provide a systematic treatment of Gestalt theory but to use gestaltists' formulation of these three issues to illumine the parables' emphasis on change through perceptual experience.

1. Perceptual Reorganization

a. *The dynamics of perceptual reorganization.* Gestalt psychologists use a number of different terms to describe the kind of perceptual reversals that Jesus' parables effect. Wertheimer termed it *recentering,* Köhler preferred the term *restructuring,* while Duncker called it *reorganization.* A good illustration of their interest in this phenomenon of perceptual reversal is the picture called Rubin's vase, named for the Danish Gestalt psychologist Edgar Rubin, who discussed it in his work. According to legend, the vase depicts the twin nephews of a Danish king who had banished the two young men and ordered all pictures and representations of them destroyed. The vase was the work of a clever Danish craftsman who claimed that anyone who saw the king's nephews in the picture was imagining things. But, of course, it can be

seen either way. Looked at one way, it appears to be a vase.
Looked at another way, it appears to be the two nephews
facing each other. This reversal is a perceptual recentering,
restructuring, or reorganization. But it is a very unstable
reorganization. The craftsman's ruse works precisely because
this is not a permanent reorganization. One's perceptions
switch from vase to nephews to vase, ad infinitum.

THE RUBIN VASE

Rubin's explanation for this perceptual instability will be
discussed later. The prior question is: What causes these
perceptual reorganizations? How is it that our original
perception of an object, phenomenon, or event may be
thoroughly reversed, so that we no longer see it as we once
did? Consider the popular parody of the Christmas hymn,
"We Three Kings of Orient Are." Some of us find it impossible to "see" the Magi as we originally saw them, before they

acquired their rubber cigars. Or consider the child who once saw hatred on his mother's face and was never able to erase this perception from his mind's eye. What causes these perceptual reorganizations?

Many cognitive and affective factors are involved in these perceptual reorganizations, but the parables themselves point to the most important factor. This is the factor of "coming to belief." As we have seen, the parables are stories about individuals coming to belief. To really "participate" in these stories, to experience the activity of God through them, meant becoming involved in this process of coming to belief. Significant perceptual reorganizations, then, are precipitated by changes in belief, and the more significant the level of belief, the more decisive the perceptual reorganization for understanding our situation in the world. Most of us today view the Rubin vase as an interesting visual anomaly, not as a phenomenon which concerns any deep level of belief. But to the Danes, the vase was a reminder of their hopes for liberation from political tyranny. For them, being able to perceive the two faces in the picture was a matter of profound belief. Similarly, there is a considerable difference in the level of belief between the perceptual reorganization that the parody of the Magi effects and the perceptual reorganization experienced by the boy who saw hatred on his mother's face. This is true in spite of the fact that the Magi are "religious figures," while the boy's encounter with his mother was a human interaction. As the parables show, the paradox of these extraordinary perceptual reversals is that they are precipitated by "ordinary" events.

When these deeper levels of belief are involved, the perceptual reorganization has a profound effect on our understanding of our situation in the world. Consider the young minister whose normal mode of perceiving the world was rudely shattered, with the result that he now saw his situation in a very different way. The encounters began in ordinary fashion—a pastoral visit to an elderly shut-in and a routine visit to an assigned ward in the state mental hospital. But then his normal expectations of what he was about to experience were suddenly challenged. The shut-in wanted to confess a sin committed thirty years ago which had ever since deprived her of peace of mind. And the young mental patient with whom he had a pleasant conversation on an earlier visit suddenly began screaming at her "voices," who were the women at church who, she believed, were condemning her for divorcing her husband. In each case, his normal mode of perceiving the world had changed. The elderly "shut-in" became a troubled "penitent," and the "attractive young patient" became a "severely disturbed psychotic." These changes in his world altered his perception of his own situation, of what was being expected or demanded of him. He was being asked to respond to the elderly woman's desire to confess her sin, and was being called on to diagnose a sick woman's spiritual problem and determine how he might help her experience healing. In the parables' view, he was being confronted with a crisis of reckoning. What previously looked like relatively routine "visits" with the two women now called for resolute, decisive action. Could he help the elderly woman gain peace of mind over her thirty-year-old sin? Could he discern not only how "religion" was contributing to the young woman's illness, but also how God could act in her life to bring healing? Undoubtedly, the young minister was being drawn into a new process of coming to belief. Not intellectual assent to concepts or ideas, but belief in God's power to transform lives. What action he took in these two situations would reveal the nature and depth of his belief in God's transforming power.

In short, two events that began with two perceptual reversals of his world—the "shut-in" becoming "penitent" and the "attractive young patient" becoming a "severely disturbed psychotic"—triggered a profound crisis of reckoning and process of coming to belief. Through this reversal, the young minister became aware of a significant change in his own situation as an individual responsible for mediating the transforming power of God to these two individuals. In Gestalt terms, his perception of his situation in the world underwent a profound reorganization. If "shut-in" became "penitent" and "attractive young patient" became "severely disturbed psychotic," he was himself changed from "casual young minister" to "mediator of God's transforming power." Thus, a perceptual reversal caused by his "world" eventuated in the reorganization of his perception of himself as one called to "minister" to the people of God.

b. *The structure of perceptual reorganization.* Thus far I have been considering perceptual reorganization from the *dynamic* point of view, focusing on the important role that coming to belief plays in effecting perceptual change. Perceptual reorganization may also be viewed from a *structural* point of view. Crossan's distinction between the parable's *literal* and *metaphorical* levels is most relevant here. As Crossan points out, Jesus' listeners needed to "see through" the literal point of the story in order to get its *metaphorical* point. Both elements of the parable are essential. The parable would not "work" if either was missing. But the metaphorical level is most important because it holds the key to the perceptual reorganization effected by the parable. The metaphorical level of the parable embodies the *activity* of God, which is why this level of the story makes the perceptual change possible. For, ultimately, it is the activity of God that triggers the perceptual reorganizations to which the parables attest.

To illustrate this point, consider Erik H. Erikson's modification of the Thematic Apperception Test (TAT) for use with children.[70] When used with adults, the TAT asks the subject to look at pictures and tell a story about them. Adapting the TAT concept for use with children, Erikson's Dramatic Productions Test asks the child to make a "scene" from the available toys and building blocks. After the scene is constructed, Erikson probes the meaning and significance of this scene for the child by asking what he calls the "dramatic question": "What is going on here?" The child responds by explaining what is happening in the scene (what the people are doing, where the cars are going, and so forth). In this case, the "action" is the metaphorical level of the child's "story." The literal level, the created scene, is not separate from the metaphorical level. On the contrary, this is the metaphorical level's means of communication, its vehicle of expression. The metaphorical level speaks through the literal level. We should therefore not exaggerate the distance between these two levels of the story, as is sometimes done when "literal" is taken to mean the "surface" story and "metaphorical" is taken to mean the "depth" dimension of the story. It is not that one is "surface" and the other "depth," but that one is verbal content while the other is the action that invigorates this content. Thus, in Erikson's Dramatic Productions Test, the point is not that there is a fundamental conflict between the literal and metaphorical meanings of the production, but that the metaphorical level tells what is really *happening* in the scene, where the dramatic *movement* is. In the same way, the metaphorical level of the parable is where the drama is going on. This level raises the dramatic question: "What is *God* doing?" And, more specifically, what is God doing in relation to the story's internal dynamic, the *coming to belief*? God may be doing any number of things, but the parable is concerned with his activity in an individual's process of coming to belief.

The suggestion that perceptual reorganization is initiated on the metaphorical level points to another Gestalt category that furthers our understanding of change through perceptual experience, the concept of *figure and ground.*

2. Figure and Ground

In classical Gestalt theory, *figure* means any discernible object, event, concept, or idea that we can bring to focus, and *ground* refers to the field or background from which the figure emerges, against which its contours are discerned, and into which the figure disappears as soon as our attention moves to some other, newly appearing figure. In Rubin's view, what makes the Rubin vase perceptually unstable is the fact that there is insufficient differentiation of figure and ground. Rubin suggested that this problem could be resolved through the use of color; the borders of the picture could be darkened, thus allowing the vase to stand out clearly as the figure. This suggests, therefore, that clarification of the figure is achieved by a change in the ground.

If we apply the figure-ground distinction to the structure of the parable, the literal or human level of the story is the figure, and the metaphorical level, the level of God's activity, is the ground. In *Patterns of Grace,* Tom F. Driver makes this very point when he talks about the relationship between man and God in terms of figure-ground relationships, and suggests that this is "a reciprocal relation. Different as they are, the one implies the other. The relation is also dynamic: knowledge requires that our attention frequently shift, focusing and refocusing, continuously forming gestalts in relation to the infinite potential of our environmental ground."[71] God's transcendence, then, is not so much the "depth" that underlies the surface of things, as Tillich suggested, but it is literally "movement across," or "the moment of hesitance between the potential ground and the actual figure." This understanding of transcendence squares with Crossan's view that the kingdom of God is not an entity but the activity of God, and that to encounter this transcendence is to experience the mystery of this activity. It also squares with the view that the "action" in perceptual reorganization originates on the metaphorical level of the story. The parable effects perceptual change because its metaphorical "ground" is not fixed, but fluid. The metaphorical point of the parables, taken as a whole, is that the dramatic question, "What is God doing?" cannot be answered confidently in advance. The ground's fluidity creates the necessary movement in the figure-ground relationship to effect perceptual reorganization. Without this movement, the relationship between figure and ground, between literal and metaphorical levels, between the human story and the activity of God, would be fixed and unchangeable. It would hold no surprises, no instability, no insecurity, and hence, no significant perceptual changes.

3. Pattern Completion

From their research on visual perception, classical gestaltists proposed the law of good continuation, which says that a perceptual pattern will complete itself, or move toward final closure, if unimpeded by factors beyond its control. In other words, the pattern has an internal drive toward completion. Thus, if we begin to draw a simple circle, our mind's eye will complete the circle even if our fingers do not. Similarly, many observers of Gilbert Stuart's unfinished portrait of George Washington "complete" this perceptual form by "seeing" the white spaces near the bottom of the portrait as clouds or billows of smoke.

Most gestaltists studied visual patterns, but a few, such as Christian von Ehrenfels, were interested in musical patterns. This latter interest is particularly suggestive for our purposes here, because much of it applies to the narrative pattern of the parables. In *Emotion and Meaning in Music,* Leonard Meyer points out that the listener's "normal expectation" is that a thematic pattern will complete itself.[72] But he also notes that, in this movement toward completion, a thematic pattern may undergo mild or severe "weakening of shape" as it seems to lose its coherence and "trembles on the brink of chaos." This weakening of shape frustrates the listener's normal expectation that the pattern will make steady progress toward completion. But it also forestalls premature closure, the formation of a trivial or excessively homogeneous pattern that holds no aesthetic interest. Moreover, this weakening of shape creates tension as it produces doubts in the listener's mind that the pattern will achieve a final, satisfying form. This period of doubt and its tension is largely responsible for creating aesthetic excitement, thus making the music "interesting" instead of "routine" or "dull." In effect, it induces greater emotional participation in the music.

Something of the same effect occurs when Jesus' parables frustrate normal expectation. Like the other rabbis of his day, Jesus could have told stories that develop and conclude in quite predictable ways. But most of his stories do not do this. They begin as though they are quite ordinary stories concerned to make a good moral point, but then something happens to disrupt the predictable narrative pattern. They "tremble on the brink of chaos" as they frustrate normal expectations of how the story will come out. In some cases, the story breaks the pattern by introducing an unexpected development, as when the unjust steward gets himself out of what appears to be a hopeless situation and is commended by his master for his clever scheme. In other cases, the expected *variation* in the pattern fails to materialize, as when the wicked husbandmen ruthlessly kill the owner's son as they had killed the two groups of servants sent before him. In these and many other parables, the thematic structure trembles on the brink of chaos, frustrating listeners' normal expectations of how the story will move toward its final conclusion.

Meyer's phrase, "tremble on the brink of chaos," is particularly apt, because Rubin observed in his studies of figure-ground relationships that the ground is more "chaotic" than the figure.[73] In a similar way, the threat of chaos in the parable occurs because the ground, the divine sphere, becomes active and makes the story be told in a different way, with a different conclusion than its opening stages seemed to require. Thus, in many parables, there are abrupt turning points in the narrative and conclusions that do not seem to fit well with what has gone before. The reason for these abrupt shifts and ill-fitting endings is that they attest to the radical disjunctures between the patterns of human experience to which we have become accustomed and the surging, brooding, mysterious ferment which we know as God's activity in human life.

B. Diagnosis and Reinterpretation in Pastoral Counseling

While classical gestaltists did not apply their theories to counseling, the potential value of their work for counseling has been recognized by a number of counselors.[74] The best known is Fritz Perls, who made use of classical gestaltists' concepts, particularly the figure-ground distinction, in developing Gestalt therapy. In a similar way, the foregoing use of classical Gestalt categories to illumine perceptual change has direct implications for a parabolic understanding of the counseling process. It has particular relevance for pastoral counseling because it provides for *diagnosis* of the counselee's situation in the light of God's activity.

Counseling involves narrative. In relating problems or troubles to the counselor, the counselee tells a story, and this story has a literal and a metaphorical level. The counselee may not be consciously aware that his or her story has a metaphorical level, but it is no less present than the literal one. In pastoral counseling, the metaphorical level is the sphere of God's activity, and is the key to the *changes* in the counselee's situation that the literal level envisions but cannot yet articulate. The pastor does not, however, dismiss the literal level to get at the metaphorical level of the story. He or she understands that both levels are meaningful, and both are as intimately bound together as figure to ground. Thus, the task is not to plumb the depths beneath the literal story, but to discern the *movement* between the literal and metaphorical levels of the story. This movement is the key to change in the counselee's situation.

The idea that discerning the movement between the two levels is the key to change is rather abstract. What does it mean in practical terms? Basically, what is involved here is *diagnosis*. Many objections have been raised against the use of diagnosis in pastoral counseling because it implies an objective, disinterested assessment of the counselee's problem. But it can also be understood as discerning the *locus* of potential movement in the counselee's story. It means asking the dramatic question: What is going on here? Where is the action? Where is the change occurring? The answer to this question requires discernment. This is the same kind of discernment that Jesus required of his listeners in using an "indirect method" of storytelling, and that Peter exhibited when he "saw through" the beggar's literal request for alms and recognized his need for wholeness. Diagnosis means discerning that point in the counselee's story where there lies the potential for significant change.

Sometimes this point is blatant and obvious. Other times it is subtle and indirect, like Jesus' metaphorical points and children's dramatic scenes. In either case, if counseling involves narrative, then the same disruptions of the thematic pattern in the parable can be found in counseling, and these disruptions signal the locus of potential change. While some counselee's narratives make steady progress toward the expected conclusion, these are the exceptional cases and, when it occurs, the counselor worries that the counselee is "covering something up." More often, a counselee's story begins by following the law of good continuation, but then something happens to disrupt the process, and the story suddenly trembles on the brink of chaos. The counselee may begin weeping, chatter nervously, have long struggling pauses, or raise the voice as the narrative thread of the story is all but lost. These are behavioral signals that the story has reached the point where the change is struggling to emerge. Literal disruptions are evidence of metaphorical movement. Put another way, they reflect the counselee's struggle against the satisfaction of normal expectations, and a yearning for the transformation of existing perceptual structures. When the story begins to "tremble on the brink of chaos," diagnostic work begins in earnest. Change is at work. The story wants to be told in a different way, and the pastor's diagnostic task is to discern the nature of the change that is struggling forth.

What kinds of change should the pastor look for? The parables suggest three possibilities. *Advent* parables suggest that the counselee may be opening up to entirely new experiences—new discoveries, new surprises, new mysteries. *Reversal* parables suggest that the counselee may be on the verge of dismantling old life structures and replacing them with new ones. *Action* parables suggest that the counselee may be preparing to take decisive action. In each case, perceptual reorganization is occurring.

A helpful guiding principle to keep in mind is that this involves reorganization of one's perception of both *self* and *world*. Let's explore the role that counseling plays in changing an individual's perception of self and world by taking a close look at one of Carl Rogers' early essays on the subject. This exploration will set the stage for our discussion of pastoral marriage counseling.[75]

C. Perceptual Reorganization in Counseling

Rogers contends that many counselees experience major "perceptual reorganizations" through the counseling process. Some have actually experienced marked changes in their visual perception of the world around them. A dramatic example is the case of Henry, an eleven-year-old boy who was referred for play therapy because of his extreme nervousness. After a great many contacts with the therapist, Henry confessed one day that when he started therapy he had many worries, but has now narrowed things down to one big worry: "how to keep myself from worrying." He told the counselor that he has "a fear that the Devil will sort of seep into my mind. I don't really believe in the Devil, but in a way I do. I'm just afraid he might seep into my mind. It's sort of a vague feeling. I can't express it."

The next week, Henry brought up the same concern, noting that he went home the previous week afraid that the Devil would punish him for telling the therapist about his fear: "So I decided to think about it. I tried to recapture my feeling about the Devil. I asked myself, 'Who is he?' And guess who he is. *Me! I* am the Devil. *I* make myself worry. All this time, the Devil has been me." This insight led to the following exchange:

THERAPIST:	So that you are your *own* Devil?
HENRY:	Exactly. I am my own Devil. All this time, I've been fighting a part of myself, using up so much of my energy to fight a part of myself, and keeping myself so tired. Using energy I could have had for other things. Say, what happened to the room?
THERAPIST:	Is there something?
HENRY:	It suddenly got lighter, like if there was a fog or a mist and an opening, and it got bigger, and the fog lifted and the mist disappeared. (Incredulously.) You mean, you don't see it?

THERAPIST: No. But things look much brighter to you now?

HENRY: Yes. It happened when I was telling it to you. It's amazing—h'm. Well, that's something. I realize now that I can think through my problems. That's something I just discovered.

This was a dramatic change in visual perception. The world became larger, lighter, clearer, and more open. This perceptual change occurred when Henry relinquished his perception of the Devil "out there" in the world and gained the insight that this "Devil" was a part of himself. Thus, the world that he had previously perceived to be threatening lost its fear-producing aspects, with the result that he could also view himself with greater confidence. Perceptual reorganization of the world "out there" was accompanied by a new self-perception. As Henry put it: "Well, that's something. I realize now that I can think through my problems."

This change in his perception of the world "out there" involved the physical environment. It was the room that got bigger and lighter. Rogers cites another case in which a counselee's changed perception of the world involved another *person.* From a psychiatric point of view, Mr. W. was "deeply paranoid," with an extreme suspiciousness of his wife when he entered therapy. But he gradually relinquished his original perception of his wife as a wicked, scheming, adulterous person. Midway through the counseling process, he began to see her as "a devoted wife who has been driven into sexual misbehavior by his own accusations growing out of his own fears regarding his sexual adequacy." While this was a major shift in his perceptions of his wife, it reflected only a partial perceptual reorganization. He still believed she was unfaithful to him. But, still later in therapy, "he had a dramatic experience—whether a dream or a type of conversion could scarcely be determined from his description—in which the whole Gestalt of his perceptions came to be viewed in a new fashion, much as the Gestalt figure in a textbook is first viewed as an ascending staircase, and now is seen as descending." This dramatic experience enabled him to relinquish his perception of her as an unfaithful wife.

The following excerpt from the counseling transcript indicates that this experience triggered a profound perceptual reorganization:

MR. W.: I had a funny experience last night that sorta turned my mind inside out. (He goes on to describe the strange quality of this dreamlike experience.) This business about my wife and Jim—that sort of blots out somehow. I can't quite straighten it out. I would like to be sure. I thought it all over. I *could* be mistaken. (Later.) I thought, too, about my wife. I put a lot of different little things together, and I realize that I might be mistaken.

COUNSELOR: It made you feel that your suspicions might not be correct.

MR. W.: That's it. I'm reasonably sure that she was right. (Later.) The sudden point in this dream, or whatever it was, was this thing about my wife. I see that I'm the one at fault there.

Rogers comments: "Here the perception has completed a full about-face. The perception of his wife as a shameless, deceitful, adulterous person has shifted completely to a perception of her as an individual devoted to him and not involved in any deceitfulness or sexual misconduct." Along with this change in his perception of his wife, Mr. W. experienced a new perception of himself which he had previously tried to avoid. Rogers continues, "Concurrently, the perception of himself as a righteous and aggrieved husband has changed to a picture of himself as having felt sexually inadequate, and as having imagined his wife's unfaithfulness."

Explaining this perceptual reorganization, Rogers stresses the importance of the therapeutic relationship in making it possible. Mr. W. was accepted as he was, with all his paranoid tendencies, and through the security this acceptance provided, he was able to risk new perceptions of himself and his wife. In a real sense, his paranoia went unsupported in his immediate therapeutic experience, and this encouraged perceptual changes that more accurately reflected the reality of his situation.

Rogers stresses the fact that such perceptual reorganizations result in greater *personal stability:* "Where the client does face more of the totality of his experience and where he adequately differentiates and symbolizes this experience, then as the new self-structure is organized it becomes firmer, more clearly defined, a steadier, more stable guide to behavior." At the same time, there is less *perceptual rigidity:* "A change in the manner of perceiving also comes about. Because there is less defensiveness, there is less perceptual rigidity. Sensory evidence can be more readily admitted to awareness. It can be interpreted and perceived in a greater variety of ways and with a greater degree of differentiation." Thus, the new self engages the world with greater confidence: "There are fewer experiences perceived as vaguely threatening. There is, consequently, much less anxiety. There is a less insistent need for closure and more tolerance of ambiguity. Thus, there is both a greater tentativeness and a greater assurance in the perceptions of the individual at the end of therapy."

In Mr. W.'s case, greater personal stability and less perceptual rigidity provided the foundation for other, positive self-perceptions as the therapeutic process continued. But, the important perceptual reversal had already occurred, and Rogers is right to wonder whether Mr. W.'s experience was "a type of conversion." Or, to put it differently, are "conversions" largely a matter of perceptual reorganization?

Because Rogers' case of Mr. W. involved a marital conflict, it provides a good point of transition for us as we begin to focus on pastoral marriage counseling. The following discussion centers on the counseling process itself, including its objectives, methods, and counselor-counselee relationship. It emphasizes perception as the focus of change in pastoral marriage counseling.

PASTORAL MARRIAGE COUNSELING

Role-Relationship Marriage Counseling

Probably the most carefully developed approach to pastoral marriage counseling is the *role relationship* model. Clinebell points out that, when two people marry, they create a new psychological entity—their relationship—and this entity becomes the focus of attention in marriage counseling.[76] Thus, pastoral marriage counseling focuses on "improving the marriage relationship, not (as in the case of uncovering psychotherapy) on resolving intrapsychic personality conflicts," and "the master goal of this approach to marriage counseling is *to make the relationship more mutually need-satisfying.*"

Charles W. Stewart also advocates the role-relationship approach in his two books, *The Minister as Marriage Counselor* and *The Minister as Family Counselor.*[77] In his view, pastoral marriage counseling is not "uncovering (insight) therapy" but "supportive therapy," which focuses on "the relationship between husband and wife" and is concerned with "the adjustment of these two persons to one another." Stewart lists the following objectives of role-relationship marriage counseling:

1. Marriage counseling is limited to *current problems* in relationships between marriage partners.

2. The counselor helps the couple to begin to *communicate feelings* to each other again.

3. The counselor helps the couple to *adjust* to certain situations in the marriage that cannot be changed, such as deeply rooted character traits.

4. The counselor helps the couple to play down personal goals and to work toward *goals that are mutually set.*

5. The counselor helps each partner *to understand the other and his or her role* in the marriage, giving each partner the opportunity to adjust to what the mate and the marriage demand.

All five goals focus on the *relationship* itself. The counseling process centers on current problems in this relationship (goal #1), and through exploration of these problems, it helps the couple communicate feelings (#2), adjust to unchangeable situations (#3), work toward mutual goals (#4), and achieve better understanding of their respective roles (#5).

Regarding the first goal of centering on current problems, Clinebell makes the valuable suggestion that this can be best achieved by focusing on specific incidents or "vignettes of interaction." When one marriage partner makes a generalized complaint against the other, the pastor says, "Let's look at a 'for instance' of that problem," and the counselee responds by providing a vignette of interaction involving the husband and wife and any other persons that may have played a role in the situation.

In my judgment, this focus on vignettes of interaction gives role-relationship counseling a parabolic thrust. The counseling session does not remain on the level of generalized complaints but centers on stories. Moreover, like the parable, these vignettes are concerned with the *relationship* between the primary actors in the story and catch the participants in *characteristic action.* The counselees tell stories that serve as examples of how they relate to each other, with the story chosen to illustrate not a once-in-a-lifetime event but a characteristic pattern of behavior. Thus, a vignette may be preceded by the comment, "It never fails . . ." or "I wish just once . . ." or "I said to myself, here we go again. . . ." And, after one has told the story, the other's defense against the relevance of the story to their marital difficulties is typically that the behavior described is uncharacteristic: "But this wasn't typical . . ." or "I only did it that once. . . ." Or, if characteristic, it is a trivial matter: "So what if I get cigarette ashes on the coffee table. They're easy enough to clean up." Or, if not trivial, why has it only now become an issue? "Maybe I don't cook fancy meals, but you didn't complain about it until the kids left home." Thus, through its vignettes of interaction, role-relationship counseling has a clear parabolic thrust. It focuses the counseling process on the relationship between individuals, it centers on characteristic actions in this relationship, and we might also say that it brings the couple to a *crisis of reckoning.* Before now, these issues could be dismissed or ignored. But now, one or both are faced with a crisis of reckoning, where characteristic patterns of behavior, and the perceptions on which they are based, are being threatened. New perceptions are struggling to take their place.

Consider the following vignette of interaction in Clinebell's case of the Blackrights. Mrs. Blackright has just related an incident in which Mr. Blackright spilled a pitcher of orange juice on the kitchen floor:

PASTOR: What happened then?

MRS. BLACKRIGHT: I came charging in, yelled at him to be more careful, and then cleaned up the mess.

PASTOR:	Why did *you* clean it up?
MRS. BLACKRIGHT:	I knew he'd take hours to get around to it, and he'd make another mess in cleaning up that one!
PASTOR:	(To Mr. Blackright) How did you feel about her cleaning up the mess?
MR. BLACKRIGHT:	She's a perfectionist! Always after me to do something! I can never do anything well enough to please her! She wouldn't have liked the way I cleaned up the floor.
PASTOR:	Anything else?
MR. BLACKRIGHT:	(with a sly smile) Well, I suppose I knew that if I waited a little while she would do it.

Like the parable, this story is about a rather mundane affair. And, like the parable, it captures the couple interacting with each other in characteristic ways. Mrs. Blackright characteristically takes charge of situations because she believes her husband will only make things worse. And Mr. Blackright characteristically lets her take over because he believes that she will only criticize his efforts to set things right. It also appears that, through such vignettes, the Blackrights are being moved toward a crisis of reckoning. Whether the orange juice episode will bring matters to a head is difficult to tell, but we can be sure that it is not bolts of lightning that trigger crises of reckoning, but just such mundane episodes as this.

How can this vignette of interaction be exploited to effect perceptual change? First, the pastor can take note of the fact that Mr. and Mrs. Blackright both have perceptions of each other—"he's messy" and "she's a perfectionist"—that they each consider to be self-evidently damning. But are these perceptions much different from saying "he's a Samaritan," and assuming that this should be prima facie evidence that he is not to be trusted? From the parabolic point of view, we cannot assume that "he's messy" or "she's a perfectionist" is a sign that this is necessarily bad or subject to condemnation. But this is only part of the problem. The deeper problem is that they assume that these perceptions of each other as messy or perfectionist are accurate. It is not difficult to see, however, that these are not very accurate or insightful perceptions. This is like seeing the man at the Beautiful Gate as a "beggar" rather than as "a man who needs to be made whole." Take Mrs. Blackright's perception of her husband as a messy person who must be cleaned up after or he may make another mess. How accurate is this? How close does it come to capturing the "real" Mr. Blackright in this episode? In his final comment, he reveals that he rather enjoys being dependent on his wife, allowing her to take charge. Thus, while he appears to his wife as a "messy" person, he reveals himself to be a "dependent" person. Conversely, while his wife appears to him to be a "perfectionist," what she reveals in this episode is not perfectionism but a strong tendency to assume responsibility for her husband. She is actually a "responsible" person. Thus, through this vignette of interaction, they reveal things about themselves that the other person cannot or will not see. Also, if they can begin to see each other more accurately, they will simultaneously see that their own self-perceptions are faulty.

What the pastor looks for here is evidence of movement at the perceptual level. Clinebell implies that the pastor in this case felt there was such movement in Mr. Blackright's acknowledgment that he knew if he waited, his wife would clean up after him. As Clinebell puts it, "This final insight was a bright ray of hope to the counselor." Whether this statement reflects real change in Mr. Blackright's self-perception is difficult to tell. He might simply have made this statement to oblige the pastor, much as he does his wife, by making the pastor feel that he is beginning to get a handle on the problem. And, even if Mr. Blackright is beginning to perceive how he and his wife relate to each other in terms of dependency and dominance, we have no evidence as yet that he plans to take decisive action based on this perception.

Still, this vignette of interaction enables the pastor to discern (diagnose) that the locus of change in their relationship concerns their tendency to relate to each other with dependency and dominance. How will the change come about? Perhaps it will come from a decisive action by one or the other—her decision not to "take charge" when a similar episode occurs or his decision to "take charge" before she has the opportunity or necessity to do so. Or maybe it will come from vignettes of interaction in the counseling process itself, as Mr. Blackright assumes responsibility for telling a story and Mrs. Blackright allows him to tell it in his own way. If this should happen, it would confirm the parabolic view that stories may actually embody perceptual change.

As these vignettes of interaction are explored, the other counseling goals in Stewart's list come into play. The counselees' efforts to describe the incident from their own points of view initiate the communication of feeling (goal #2). The pastor's role here is to discern the kinds and intensity of feelings that are communicated in the counselees' conversation about the incident. Goal #3, helping the couple to adjust to certain situations that cannot be changed, is also addressed through vignettes of interaction. By exploring such incidents with the couple, the pastor helps them determine what can be changed in the way they relate to each other, and what is likely to be unchangeable and thus require readjustment.

In my view, the parabolic understanding of counseling is particularly relevant to this goal #3. For, while Stewart emphasizes adjustment to what cannot be changed, marriage counseling based on the parables is particularly concerned with identifying where real change is possible. As emphasized earlier, the pastor wants to identify the locus of the counselee's potential for change, particularly in the area of perceptual reorganization. In the parabolic approach to marriage counseling, the pastor attends to both the literal and metaphorical level of vignettes of interaction. Listening to these vignettes and the counselee's conversation about them, the pastor discerns the potential for perceptual reorganization in the marriage relationship. The parabolic approach emphasizes change not because it is more starry-eyed about the couple's marriage relationship, but because it recognizes that changes in perception are changes in fact. What Stewart sees as "adjustment" to what cannot be changed can be viewed as a new way of perceiving the couple's relatively fixed patterns of interaction.

Consider the husband who was resentful of his wife because she earned a larger salary than he did. After pastoral marriage counseling, the fact that she makes more than he does no longer troubled him. Was this because he adjusted to what could not be changed? Or was it because his perception of the situation was reorganized? Adjustment implies resignation to the fact that his wife's salary exceeds his own. But perceptual reorganization means a reversal in the way he sees the whole situation.

The first thing that the pastoral conversation did was to help Mr. Reeves recall that he had chosen his lower paying occupation twenty years earlier because it had special, intrinsic rewards. Partly because he was blinded by his resentment toward his wife, he had since forgotten some of his reasons for choosing this occupation, but counseling helped him remember and rekindle his earlier feelings toward the occupation that he had chosen. The second thing that the conversation accomplished was to provide the impetus for talking with his wife about his resentment. She was surprised to hear that he had felt this way, and pointed out that one reason she was attracted to him twenty years ago was that he had chosen his occupation not for financial reasons, but because he liked the work and was good at it. She also recalled how her own father spent his whole working life changing from one job to another, and that she had wanted a husband whose work life was more stable. She also observed that, because her husband was personally secure in his work, she had felt free to go back to college after the children were grown in order to pursue her own professional goals. This conversation led to renewed appreciation for the fact that their marriage was based not on competition but on mutual support and encouragement. When Mr. Reeves reported this conversation to his pastor, he added: "I feel a whole lot differently about my wife's salary. After all, we're working for the same goals, and she appreciates what I've done to help her get her professional start. The thing that impressed me the most, though, was how she compared me so favorably to her own father. I had always felt she worshiped the ground he walked on, and believed I could never measure up to him. But, now, after all these years, I feel like I'm the 'big man' in her eyes. It's real gratifying."

Mr. Reeves has not merely adjusted to the fact that his wife has a larger salary than his. Rather, his whole perception of this situation has changed. There has been a perceptual reorganization of his world, particularly in his view of his occupational choice (physical environment) and his wife (other person), and this is reflected in a change in his perception of himself ("big man"). This perceptual reorganization has not changed the situation that gave rise to his resentment—his wife's higher salary—but his situation has nonetheless undergone a major transformation. He is now able to set aside personal resentment and to see his marriage relationship in terms of *mutual goals,* as reflected in his earlier contribution to his wife's pursuit of her professional goals (goal #4 in Stewart's schema). The couple also reflect on improved understanding of their *respective roles,* as shown in the importance his wife attaches to his occupational stability (goal #5 in Stewart's list). Thus, this example indicates that the perceptual reorganization (alternative to adjustment in goal #3) was responsible for achieving goals #4 and #5.

In short, the parabolic approach to pastoral marriage counseling gives central importance to the role that perception plays in changing the marriage relationship. This does not mean that it downplays the communication of *feelings* (goal #2) or *behavioral changes* reflected in the adoption of mutual goals (goal #4) or new roles (goal #5). But it does mean that perception is viewed as the primary agent of change.

Marriage Failure

In premarital counseling, the pastor helps the couple develop grounds for confidence that a marriage in which the two partners act wisely and virtuously will be blessed. Thus, premarital counseling reflects the normal expectation that wisdom and virtue are rewarded, and that these rewards are, in a certain sense, self-generating. But for many persons who are experiencing serious marital difficulties, such confidence no longer sustains them, and for many who are going through separation and divorce, it has long since given way to bitter recriminations and distrust, and any sense of moral commitment to one another is all but destroyed. Any sense of moral purpose that still survives is directed toward protecting children who are the "victims" of their parents' incompatibility.

This situation is not unlike the situations that Jesus portrayed in his parables, where the usual moral order that sustains human relationships has broken down, and individuals, as individuals, are confronted with a crisis of reckoning calling for decisive action. Consider the following case of a promising marriage relationship that, within the space of only three years, was ending in divorce.

Pete was an accountant in his middle twenties who, after three years of marriage, had just filed for divorce. Over the course of the previous twelve months, his marriage to Stephanie had deteriorated. About a year ago, Stephanie suddenly had begun seeing another man whom she had met at work. At first she succeeded in deceiving Pete. After two or three months, Pete caught on, and was both angry and hurt. He had no prior reason to suspect that there was anything wrong with their marriage relationship and when he asked Stephanie why she was being unfaithful, she said that she didn't know, that she had nothing against Pete and still loved him, but she also enjoyed being in Jerry's company. She promised Pete that she would quit seeing Jerry, and for the next seven months it seemed the crisis was over. Pete was still deeply hurt by Stephanie's infidelity, but his anger subsided, and he was genuinely relieved that she had decided to stay with him and no longer see Jerry. Trust began to be rebuilt as they went on a number of skiing trips together and discussed plans for moving out of the apartment into their own home.

But then the same thing happened again. Stephanie became involved with another man at work. About six weeks after discovering the new problem Pete met with Pastor Lynd over lunch to talk with her about his marriage. Pete had pleaded with his wife to go with him to see Pastor Lynd or a marriage counselor, but she was unwilling to go. After vainly trying to come to an understanding with his wife, who admitted her confusion, Pete gave up in despair and filed for divorce. A couple of days later, he asked to see Pastor Lynd because he "wanted to be sure that he had done everything in his power to save his marriage."

As the pastoral conversation focused on the marriage relationship that was soon to be legally dissolved, Pete contrasted his feelings about his marriage now with the way he felt at the time he and Stephanie were married: "When she and I were first married, I thought I knew what I could expect. I knew things wouldn't be all rosy, but I was confident we would have a good marriage. Now, I know how wrong I was. It has not turned out at all like I thought it would." He continued: "I tried hard to make this marriage work. I tried to be understanding of Stephanie and her needs. I believe I honestly forgave her for her affair with Jerry and didn't use it against her. . . . But it didn't do much good. I tried hard to save our marriage, but I guess I've failed."

Pete did not claim that his role in the marriage was always what it should have been. But he had hoped that by making a serious effort to make their marriage work after trouble started, he would be able to save it.

Pete's pride was very much involved in his effort to save his marriage. But Pastor Lynd felt that what Pete was experiencing, even more than an assault to his pride, was his loss of confidence in life's basic fairness. Pete believed that his understanding attitude toward Stephanie, and their efforts to work toward mutual goals, would enable them to reestablish their marriage on a basis of mutual trust. So he was genuinely mystified, frustrated, and irritated that these efforts had failed. As he expressed it to Pastor Lynd: "Many times during the past few weeks I doubted that God cared whether my marriage survived or not."

Pastor Lynd knew that her role was not to voice suspicions about Pete's motives for wanting to save his marriage, but to respond with empathy and understanding, for Pete was clearly lamenting the breakdown of his marriage. On the other hand, she recognized that her counseling objectives needed to go beyond providing solace, essential as that was to the healing process, that her task was somehow to help Pete come to terms with the failure of his efforts to save his marriage. Right now, this failure disturbed him more than anything else. What Pete needed was to see his situation in a radically new way.

Pastor Lynd believed that this perception would have to come from some new understanding of how God was active in the recent events in Pete's life. This meant probing the metaphorical level of Pete's story, and asking the dramatic question: Where is the action in Pete's story? Where is the *locus* of potential change? She thought of the possibility that Pete could go back to Stephanie and make one last effort to save his marriage. But he had tried this approach and it had failed. The potential for change did not appear to lie in that direction. In fact, it was difficult to see any potential for change in anything Pete might try to work out with Stephanie. The potential for change must be in another direction. But where?

Pete's reason for wanting to talk with Pastor Lynd—"to make sure I have done everything in my power to save our marriage"—provided the clue. The change needed to take place here, and it needed to begin with Pete's *perception* of his situation. This perception needed to be changed. He needed to see that the locus of action had shifted. While Pete's power was concentrated on saving his marriage, *God* was active differently.

This perceptual change began to develop toward the end of the counseling hour. Pete said: "Now I begin to sense that deciding to let this marriage go is a bigger step than getting married. But, you know, another thought has been dawning on me. This is that somehow this divorce is going to be good for me. A promising marriage, and now, a good divorce. I know it sounds crazy."

This perception of divorce as a good thing for him, as something positive, was a whole new way of looking at the situation. But, as Pete allowed it to take hold, it felt right to him. Before, divorce was something to fear, a sign of personal and moral weakness. But now Pete found himself beginning to embrace it. As Pete and the minister stood up and prepared to leave the restaurant, he said: "When I went to file the divorce papers, I remember thinking that what I most feared would happen this whole year is now happening. And yet, I'm the one who is actually doing it, taking the initiative!"

This resolution of Pete's feelings also felt right to Pastor Lynd. Yes, she wished that Pete and Stephanie could have worked out their difficulties. And yes, she wished Pete had come to her earlier, before the situation had gone so far, because she might have been able to help restore the marriage. But she saw promise in Pete's emerging perception that the divorce would be good for him, and was glad that he felt reassured in this new understanding. It relieved her that toward the end of the session Pete had stopped worrying whether he'd done enough to try to save his marriage. She honestly believed that his perception that his divorce would be good for him was a reflection of God's activity in his life.

But subsequently she remembered the evening she had officiated at their wedding and pondered: Why do I feel this way about Pete's divorce? Have I gotten soft on divorce? Have I begun to accept society's casual attitude about divorce, as though it were no longer a moral issue? But if so, I doubt that I would have felt that Pete's anger was justified concerning Stephanie's infidelity. I felt hurt for him when he told me these things. I was disappointed at the failure of a marriage I helped create. No, I've not gone soft on divorce. Then what is it? What made me accept the fact that Pete won't be trying to save his marriage or justify its failure, and is coming to the belief that divorce will be genuinely good for him? And what makes me now believe that God is behind this change in Pete's perception of the situation?

The answer was profound in its simplicity: Pete's emerging perception of his divorce as "good," when he had previously viewed it as "bad," was a participation in the Parable of God.

What enabled him to see divorce as "good" was similar to what happened to Jesus' followers after he was killed. Jesus had been defeated, rejected by God. But was this the only way his death could be envisioned? Could it be seen from a different point of view? By discerning that the cross was God's Parable, their perception of his death was reversed— it was not defeat but victory, not cause for despair but grounds for hope. They did not come to this perception merely by reflecting on his death. They suffered with him, participating in his death as though it were their own, and it was out of this experience that their perception of his death was changed.

In the past few weeks, Pete experienced the death of his marriage relationship, and something in him died as well. He would have little difficulty comparing his dead marriage to a cross, or his current situation to that of the disciples for whom the unthinkable and the unimaginable had happened. He naturally believed that God was on his side when he was trying to keep his marriage alive, and it would be natural to think that God has abandoned him now that he has filed for divorce. But this is to assume that God plays the game according to our rules. If Jesus' parable linked Good + Samaritan, Pete's perception that divorce might be the better solution was a process of coming to belief. This was not intellectual assent, but a new sense of how God may act through the experience of marriage failure.

The Untimeliness of Marriage Counseling

Pete came to Pastor Lynd after he had filed the divorce papers. This sequence is common in pastoral marriage counseling. In contrast to premarital and grief counseling, where the pastor is able to give counsel at the "proper" time, marriage counseling is often frustrating because it seems to come too late to do much good. Pastors often complain: "Why was

I consulted so late? Why did the couple wait so long before seeking help? Why did I have to discover problems from a third party?"[78] I would like to comment briefly on the untimeliness of marriage counseling by taking note of the "It May Be Too Late" parables of Jesus, thereby concluding our analysis of Pete's failed marriage.

In these parables, Jesus extends his critique of our confidence in the *moral* order to the *temporal* order. The literal point of these parables is that "it may be too late," but their metaphorical point is that God's activity is most evident when the time seems to have run out. Pastoral marriage counseling is *inherently* untimely. Conceivably, it would have helped if Pete had come for counseling much earlier, before the problem became so intractable and before he had taken definite steps to end his marriage. But in pastoral marriage counseling, the very notion of the "proper" time or the "seasonable" moment is a fundamental misperception. Pastoral marriage counseling is effective not because it confronts marital conflicts at the "proper" time, but because it recognizes that God is active in the untimeliness of marital conflict. Thus, Pastor Lynd would have been as pleased as Pete himself if she could have helped to save his marriage. But the issue is not that it was "too late" to save Pete's marriage, but whether more wholistic perceptions of life emerge from the experience of marital conflict. Pete's perception of his divorce as "good" would have been morally disturbing to Pastor Lynd were it not for the fact that it enabled him to perceive *himself* as neither a psychological nor a moral cripple, but as a whole man, alive to the future where God was already active.

CONCLUSION

Pastoral counseling informed by the parables views the counseling process in narrative terms. The *counselor-coun-*

selee relationship is based on the understanding that the counselor listens with diagnostic sensitivity to the story the counselee tells. This is not a passive listening, but listening like that of those who are hearing Jesus' stories for the first time, for whom listening means active participation in the story. Erik Erikson's view of counseling as "disciplined subjectivity" gets at this sense of listening as both *discernment* and *participation.* [79]

The counseling *objectives* and *methods* of pastoral conversation informed by the parables are based on the fact that the counselee's narrative has a metaphorical level, and that in pastoral conversation this metaphorical level is understood as the activity of God. Thus, the counseling objectives reflect awareness that God is the ultimate *ground* of perceptual reorganization, and the methods are *in* directive because the ultimate focus of this counseling, the activity of God, is filtered through stories of ordinary, mundane, "secular" experience. In the parables, there are no direct references to God, and there is no basis for identifying God with any of the protagonists in the stories, including the father in the parable of the Prodigal Son, the vineyard owner in the parable of the Vineyard Workers, or the father in the parable of the Wicked Husbandmen.

Thus, whether God is actually referred to in the conversation depends on the circumstances, not on the supposition that conversation without talk about God is somehow less than pastoral. But it *is* essential that the conversation be sensitive to how God is acting in the counselee's situation. Jesus' parables have no meaning apart from their reference to the activity of God. In the same way, the major purpose of pastoral conversation informed by the parables is to discern God's activity in human lives.

I have talked about how the parables, taken as a whole, inform the counseling process. What about individual parables? Are particular parables especially relevant to problems confronted in marriage counseling? In the two previous chapters, I provided examples of specific psalms and proverbs that may be used in grief and premarital counseling. I hesitate to follow the same procedure here, for this could resurrect the view that Jesus' parables are moral tales or allegories. The Judge and the Importunate Widow might be used to illustrate how men should deal with their wives, or the parable of the Sower might serve as an allegory for contrasting good and bad marriage relationships! On the other hand, I believe that it is legitimate and genuinely helpful to relate the three major *types* of parables to pastoral marriage counseling. For, in effect, marriage consists of three major modalities: *advent, reversal,* and *action.*

Viewed in terms of *advent,* the marriage relationship is always in the process of becoming. While it is currently popular to talk about this process in terms of "growth," the advent parables see this "growth" in terms of "miracles of grace." The themes that Jesus chose to portray these miracles are most relevant to marriage, for they focus on *hiddenness and mystery, gift and surprise,* and *discovery and joy.* These themes can help the pastor diagnose the kinds of "growth" that need to be cultivated in the counselee's marriage relationship.

The marriage relationship is also threatened with unanticipated *reversals.* Reversal parables draw attention to a feature of human experience that is perhaps felt most profoundly in the marriage relationship, the fact that some reversals in life are experienced as complete or "polar" reversals. A violent argument or a single breach of trust can cause both partners to feel as though, in Crossan's apt image, "the north pole becomes the south pole, and the south the north, a world is reversed and overturned and we find ourselves standing firmly on utter uncertainty." Thus, while the major trend of a marriage relationship may be in the direction of steady growth, few marriages are not threatened by these unexpected and complete reversals, where the participants question whether the relationship is worth maintaining at all.

Action parables focus on the moment of decision, and this too is an important feature of marriage. Failure to take firm and resolute action in matters directly affecting the marriage relationship is often the cause of marital conflict. A complaint commonly heard by marriage counselors is that a spouse refuses to take action, as in the case of a teenage son who is beginning to run with the wrong crowd, or cannot make important decisions, including the failure to "do something" about a deteriorating marriage relationship before it is "too late." Jesus' action parables are more critical of indecision than of decisions that prove misguided, and they issue a challenge to married couples to take risks and dare to make themselves vulnerable. According to Crossan, these parables tell us that it is in making ourselves vulnerable that "God can touch us."

These three types of parables have direct relevance for marriage counseling. Instead of looking to individual parables for examples of how to conduct a marriage relationship, it is more in keeping with the intention of the parables that we view them as means of sensitizing us to the three major modalities in married life: advent, reversal, and decision. Also, the *resurrection* stories in the Gospels are particularly valuable for sensitizing us to the role of perception in these three modalities. For, like Jesus' own experience of God, his disciples' experiences of the risen Christ were clearly perceptual in nature. One thinks here of the Road to Emmaus story where the disciples' "eyes were opened and they recognized him" (Luke 24:31), or of the Empty Tomb story, where the women's normal expectations of anointing the body of Jesus were dashed, and his followers began to "see" him instead as the risen Lord. The Empty Tomb story is particularly relevant to the perceptual reorganizations that occur in pastoral marriage counseling. Many pastors have vividly etched in their memories the perplexity and incomprehension of a parishioner who has begun to realize that his or her marriage is nothing but an empty tomb. As the resurrection stories attest, what this parishioner "sees" in the emptiness of the tomb will make all the difference in the world.

Epilogue:
Metaphor
in Pastoral Counseling

By focusing on three different biblical forms in this study, I have taken the view that there is no single biblical perspective that applies to all pastoral counseling situations. Different biblical forms relate to different types of pastoral counseling situations, and generate different counseling methods, different ways of understanding the counselor-counselee relationship, and different counseling objectives. This diversity frustrates efforts to formulate *the* biblical approach to pastoral counseling.

On the other hand, the three approaches discussed in this study do not reflect a fragmented understanding of the Bible's role in pastoral counseling. The three approaches developed here are based on biblical forms that are similar in their attention to metaphor, and this gives them a certain unity in diversity. Psalms and proverbs do not share the parable's narrative form, but they make considerable use of metaphors. Moreover, all three employ metaphors that reflect a common theme of human experience, the sense that one has of being disoriented in one's world.

Metaphors in the psalms typically reflect an important dimension of this theme, the experience of *transition.* One walks through the valley of the shadow of death (Psalm 23), one is drawn up from the miry bog (Psalm 40), one is like a leaning wall or a tottering fence, about to be brought down (Psalm 62), and people are like grass that flourishes in the morning and fades and withers by evening (Psalm 90). Many other transition metaphors could be cited, but these few make the point that, for the psalms, we live between the times, and seek God in the process of moving from one secure point to another.

Metaphors in the proverbs reflect another dimension of this theme of disorientation, the quest for *permanence and stability.* Thus: "Wisdom has built her house, she has set up her seven pillars" (Prov. 9:1); "The wicked are overthrown and are no more, but the house of the righteous will stand" (12:7); "The strong tower of the wicked comes to ruin, but the root of the righteous stands firm" (12:12); and "A man without self-control is like a city broken into and left without walls" (25:28). These metaphors, and many others like them, indicate that the proverbs are concerned with permanence and stability. They draw attention to our desire to establish our life on firm, reliable foundations, to make the universe a home.

Metaphors in the parables reflect a third dimension of this disorientation theme, the insecurity of *radical change.* The mustard seed becomes a huge shrub (Mark 4:30–32), the rich fool suddenly dies (Luke 12:16–20), a man's discovery of a hidden treasure completely alters his life (Matt. 13:44), and a steward suddenly finds himself threatened with the loss of his job (Luke 16:1–9). There are many other examples in the parables of metaphors that reflect radical change, but these indicate Jesus' understanding of the insecurity of human life, the sense, as Crossan puts it, of "standing firmly on utter uncertainty."

These metaphorical preferences support the view developed in this study that some psalms may be especially relevant to *grief counseling* (death being the most threatening and disturbing *transition* that humans can possibly experience), proverbs are useful in *premarital counseling* (when couples are seeking to establish their lives on a *firm and reliable foundation*), and parables can help in *marriage counseling* (when couples find themselves facing the opportunity and threat of *radical change*). While these three biblical forms favor different types of metaphors, what unites them is their use of metaphors to deal with our sense of disorientation in this world. Thus, their application to pastoral counseling is most appropriate because, more than any other ministerial function, pastoral counseling is concerned with the individual's sense of disorientation in the world. In other words, pastoral counseling assumes responsibility for helping individuals cope with situations that cause disorientation—situations that force them to the limits of their endurance, moral insight, and comprehension.

Notes

1. Clifford E. Geertz, "Religion as a Cultural System," in *The Interpretation of Cultures* (Basic Books, 1973), pp. 87–125.

2. Richard C. Cabot and Russell L. Dicks, *The Art of Ministering to the Sick* (Macmillan Co., 1936), Ch. 17.

3. This view is expressed in such publications as Russell L. Dicks, *Pastoral Work and Personal Counseling* (Macmillan Co., 1944), *Meditations for the Sick* (Willett, Clark & Co., 1937), and *Principles and Practices of Pastoral Care* (Prentice-Hall, 1963), Ch. 9.

4. Seward Hiltner, *Pastoral Counseling* (Abingdon-Cokesbury Press, 1949), Ch. 9.

5. Wayne E. Oates, *The Bible in Pastoral Care* (Westminster Press, 1953).

6. Edgar Draper, *Psychiatry and Pastoral Care* (Prentice-Hall, 1965).

7. Carroll A. Wise, *Psychiatry and the Bible* (Harper & Brothers, 1956).

8. Heije Faber and Ebel van der Schoot, *The Art of Pastoral Conversation* (Abingdon Press, 1965).

9. Eduard Thurneysen, *A Theology of Pastoral Care,* trans. Jack A. Worthington and Thomas Wieser (John Knox Press, 1962), Chs. 5–8.

10. Thomas C. Oden, *Contemporary Theology and Psychotherapy* (Westminster Press, 1967), Ch. 5.

11. Howard J. Clinebell, Jr., *Basic Types of Pastoral Counseling* (Abingdon Press, 1966).

12. Gary R. Collins, *Effective Counseling* (Creation House, 1972).

13. Jay E. Adams, *Competent to Counsel* (Presbyterian & Reformed Publishing Co., 1972), and *The Use of the Scriptures in Counseling* (Presbyterian & Reformed Publishing Co., 1977).

14. John B. Cobb, Jr., *Theology and Pastoral Care* (Fortress Press, 1977).

15. David K. Switzer, *Pastor, Preacher, Person: Developing a Pastoral Ministry in Depth* (Abingdon Press, 1979).

16. William B. Oglesby, Jr., *Biblical Themes for Pastoral Care* (Abingdon Press, 1980).

17. William B. Oglesby, Jr., "Pastoral Care and Counseling in Biblical Perspective," *Interpretation,* Vol. 27, pp. 307–326.

18. Paul W. Pruyser, *The Minister as Diagnostician: Personal Problems in Pastoral Perspective* (Westminster Press, 1976), p. 95.

19. See Gene M. Tucker, *Form Criticism of the Old Testament* (Fortress Press, 1971), p. 34.

20. My *Pastoral Care: A Thematic Approach* (Westminster Press, 1979) develops principles for such interpretation.

21. Hiltner, *Pastoral Counseling,* Ch. 9.

22. Wise, *Psychiatry and the Bible,* pp. 11ff.

23. Oates, *The Bible in Pastoral Care,* Ch. 5.

24. Seward Hiltner, *The Christian Shepherd: Some Aspects of Pastoral Care* (Abingdon Press, 1959), Ch. 2.

25. Bernhard W. Anderson, *Out of the Depths: The Psalms Speak for Us Today* (Westminster Press, 1974), pp. 54–56.

26. Claus Westermann, *The Psalms: Structure, Content and Message,* trans. Ralph D. Gehrke (Augsburg Publishing Company, 1980), and "The Role of the Lament in the Theology of the Old Testament," *Interpretation,* Vol. 28, pp. 20–38.

27. William Bridges, *A Lifting Up for the Downcast* (Banner of Truth Trust, 1961).

28. Harvey Seifert and Howard J. Clinebell, Jr., *Personal Growth and Social Change* (Westminster Press, 1969), and Wayne E. Oates, *Pastoral Counseling in Social Problems* (Westminster Press, 1966).

29. See Gaylord B. Noyce, "Has Ministry's Nerve Been Cut by

the Pastoral Counseling Movement?" *The Christian Century,* Feb. 1-8, 1978, pp. 103-114.

30. Walter Brueggemann, "The Formfulness of Grief," *Interpretation,* Vol. 31, pp. 263-275. See also his earlier article on the lament, "From Hurt to Joy, From Death to Life," *Interpretation,* Vol. 28, pp. 3-19.

31. Elisabeth Kübler-Ross, *On Death and Dying* (Macmillan Co., 1969).

32. Other stage theories include Granger Westberg, *Good Grief: A Constructive Approach to the Problem of Loss* (Fortress Press, 1962), and Wayne E. Oates, *Pastoral Care and Counseling in Grief and Separation* (Fortress Press, 1976).

33. Newman S. Cryer, Jr., and John M. Vayhinger (eds.), *Casebook in Pastoral Counseling* (Abingdon Press, 1962), pp. 71-73.

34. David K. Switzer, *The Minister as Crisis Counselor* (Abingdon Press, 1974), p. 148.

35. Cryer and Vayhinger, *Casebook in Pastoral Counseling,* pp. 63-65.

36. James E. Dittes, *When the People Say No: Conflict and the Call to Ministry* (Harper & Row, 1979), Ch. 1.

37. Seward Hiltner, *The Counselor in Counseling* (Abingdon Press, 1957), p. 15.

38. See, for example, Adams' misrepresentation of Oates's views in *The Use of the Scriptures in Counseling,* pp. 206-207.

39. James L. Crenshaw (ed.), *Studies in Ancient Israelite Wisdom* (KTAV Publishing House, 1976), pp. 1-3.

40. J. Coert Rylaarsdam, *The Proverbs, Ecclesiastes, The Song of Solomon* (The Layman's Bible Commentary) (John Knox Press, 1964).

41. John Mark Thompson, *The Form and Function of Proverbs in Ancient Israel* (The Hague: Mouton & Co., 1974), p. 4.

42. Gerhard von Rad, *Wisdom in Israel,* trans. James D. Martin (London: SCM Press, 1972), Chs. 7-8, 12.

43. Charles William Stewart, *The Minister as Marriage Counselor,* rev. ed. (Abingdon Press, 1970), p. 52.

44. Clinebell, *Basic Types of Pastoral Counseling,* Ch. 11.

45. Robert F. Stahmann and William J. Hiebert, *Premarital Counseling* (Lexington Books, 1980).

46. Cryer and Vayhinger, *Casebook in Pastoral Counseling,* p. 78.

47. Stewart, *The Minister as Marriage Counselor,* pp. 65–66.

48. See the premarital counseling case on "mutual rights" in my earlier book, *Pastoral Care: A Thematic Approach,* pp. 98–107.

49. Clinebell, *Basic Types of Pastoral Counseling,* p. 190.

50. J. Coert Rylaarsdam, *Revelation in Jewish Wisdom Literature* (University of Chicago Press, 1946), pp. 32–33, 94–95.

51. See Don S. Browning, *The Moral Context of Pastoral Care* (Westminster Press, 1976), for further discussion of this issue.

52. Erik H. Erikson, "Human Strength and the Cycle of Generations," in *Insight and Responsibility* (W. W. Norton & Co., 1964), pp. 111–132.

53. Lawrence Kohlberg, "Continuities and Discontinuities in Childhood and Adult Moral Development," *Human Development,* Vol. 12 (1969), pp. 93–120.

54. See discussions of these further developments in Mary M. Wilcox, *Developmental Journey* (Abingdon Press, 1979), and essays by Lawrence Kohlberg, James Fowler, and others in Christiane Brusselmans (ed.), *Toward Moral and Religious Maturity* (Silver Burdett Co., 1980).

55. James Rest, "New Approaches in the Assessment of Moral Judgment," in Thomas Lickona (ed.), *Moral Development and Behavior* (Holt, Rinehart & Winston, 1976).

56. See Stahmann and Hiebert, *Premarital Counseling,* Ch. 5.

57. Wilcox, *Developmental Journey.* See also Robert L. Selman, "Taking Another's Perspective: Role-Taking Development in Early Childhood," *Child Development,* Vol. 42 (1971), pp. 1721–1734.

58. See note 49, above.

59. Robert F. Peck and Robert J. Havighurst, *The Psychology of Character Development* (John Wiley & Sons, 1960). Also see A. William Kay's *Moral Development* (Schocken Books, 1968) for a critical evaluation of this theory.

60. Erikson, "Human Strength and the Cycle of Generations," in *Insight and Responsibility;* Donald Evans, *Struggle and Fulfillment: The Inner Dynamics of Religion and Morality* (Fortress Press, 1981).

61. Wilcox, *Developmental Journey.* See chart on inside back cover.

62. Wise, *Psychiatry and the Bible,* pp. 150–152, 109–114.

63. Oates, *The Bible in Pastoral Care,* pp. 85ff.

64. James E. Dittes, *The Church in the Way* (Charles Scribner's Sons, 1967), *The Minister on the Spot* (Pilgrim Press, 1970), and *When the People Say No.*

65. Dittes is probably influenced here by James Hillman's chapter on perception in *Re-Visioning Psychology* (Harper & Row, 1975).

66. John Dominic Crossan, *In Parables: The Challenge of the Historical Jesus* (Harper & Row, 1973), p. 85.

67. Sallie McFague TeSelle, *Speaking in Parables* (Fortress Press, 1975).

68. C. S. Lewis, quoted by Crossan, *In Parables,* p. 12.

69. Paul Ricoeur, "Listening to the Parables of Jesus," in *The Philosophy of Paul Ricoeur,* ed. Charles E. Reagan and David Stewart (Beacon Press, 1978), Ch. 16.

70. Erik H. Erikson, "Dramatic Productions Test," in Henry A. Murray and others, *Explorations in Personality* (Oxford University Press, 1938), pp. 552–582.

71. Tom F. Driver, *Patterns of Grace: Human Experience as Word of God* (Harper & Row, 1977), Ch. 6.

72. Leonard Meyer, *Emotion and Meaning in Music* (University of Chicago Press, 1956).

73. See Bruno Petermann, *The Gestalt Theory and the Problem of Configuration* (London: Kegan Paul, Trench, Trubner & Co., 1932), p. 141.

74. One of the best books on Gestalt therapy is Erving Polster and Miriam Polster, *Gestalt Therapy Integrated: Contours of Theory and Practice* (Brunner/Mazel, 1973).

75. Carl R. Rogers, "Perceptual Reorganization in Client-Centered Therapy," in *Perception: An Approach to Personality,* ed. Robert R. Blake and Glenn V. Ramsey (Ronald Press Co., 1951), pp. 307–327.

76. Clinebell, *Basic Types of Pastoral Counseling,* p. 101.

77. Stewart, *The Minister as Marriage Counselor,* Ch. 7. Also see his *The Minister as Family Counselor* (Abingdon Press, 1979).

78. Wayne E. Oates points out that the pastor is not likely to be made aware of a serious marital problem until the fourth stage in a seven stage process of marital separation. See *Pastoral Care and Counseling in Grief and Separation,* pp. 24–33.

79. Erik H. Erikson, "The Nature of Clinical Evidence," in *Insight and Responsibility,* pp. 49–80.